DEADLY DERBYSHIRE

TRUE CRIME FROM WHARNCLIFFE

Foul Deeds and Suspicious Deaths Series

Barking, Dagenham and
  Chadwell Heath
Barnet, Finchley and Hendon
Barnsley
Bath
Bedford
Birmingham
Black Country
Blackburn and Hyndburn
Bolton
Bradford
Brighton
Bristol
Cambridge
Cardiff
Carlisle
Chesterfield
Colchester
Cotswolds
Coventry
Crewe
Croydon
Cumbria
Derby
Doncaster
Dublin
Durham
Ealing
Fens
Folkestone and Dover

Glasgow
Grimsby and Cleethorpes
Guernsey
Guildford
Halifax
Hampstead, Holburn and
  St Pancras
Huddersfield
Hull
Isle of Wight
Islington
Jersey
Kensington and Chelsea
Leeds
Leicester
Lewisham and Deptford
Liverpool
London's East End
London's West End
Manchester
Mansfield
More Foul Deeds Barnsley
More Foul Deeds Birmingham
More Foul Deeds Chesterfield
More Foul Deeds Wakefield
Newcastle
Newport
Norfolk
Northampton
Nottingham

Oxfordshire
Pontefract and Castleford
Portsmouth
Reading
Richmond and Kingston
Rochdale
Rotherham
Scunthorpe
Sheffield
Shrewsbury and Around
  Shropshire
South Yorkshire
Southampton
Southend-on-Sea
Southport
Staffordshire and the Potteries
Stratford and South
  WarwickshireSuffolk
Swansea
Tees
The Fens
Uxbridge
Wakefield
Warwickshire
West Riding of Yorkshire
Wigan
Worcester
York
Yorkshire Coast

OTHER TRUE CRIME BOOKS FROM WHARNCLIFFE

Black Barnsley
Brighton Crime and Vice 1800–2000
Britain's Most Notorious Hangmen
Crafty Crooks and Conmen
Criminal Women
DNA Crime Investigations
Durham Executions
Enemies of the State
Essex Murders
Executions & Hangings in Newcastle & Morpeth
Great Hoaxers, Artful Fakers and Cheating
  Charlatans
Great Train Crimes
Hanged in Lancashire
Kent Murder and Mayhem
Jack the Ripper: Quest for a Killer
Miscarriages of Justice
Murder and Mayhem in North London
Norfolk Mayhem and Murder
Norwich Murders
Notorious Murders of the Twentieth Century
Rotherham Murders
Scotland Yards's Ghost Squad
Serial Killers: Butchers and Cannibals

Serial Killers: Murder Without Mercy
Serial Killers: The World's Most Evil
Strangeways: A Century of Hangings in
  Manchester
The A-Z of London Murders
The Guv'nors
The Plot to Kill Lloyd George
The Romford Outrage
The Sweeney
The Thames Torso Murders
The Wharncliffe A-Z of Yorkshire Murder
Unsolved East Anglian Murders
Unsolved London Murders: The 1920s and 1930s
Unsolved London Murders: The 1940s and 1950s
Unsolved Murders in and Around Derbyshire
Unsolved Murders in Victorian & Edwardian
  London
Unsolved Norfolk Murders
Unsolved Yorkshire Murders
War Crimes
Warwickshire's Murderous Women
Yorkshire's Hangmen
Yorkshire's Multiple Killers
Yorkshire's Murderous Women

Please contact us via any of the methods below for more information
or a catalogue
WHARNCLIFFE BOOKS
47 Church Street, Barnsley, South Yorkshire, S70 2AS
Tel: 01226 734555 • 734222 • Fax: 01226 734438
email: enquiries@pen-and-sword.co.uk
website: www.wharncliffebooks.co.uk

DEADLY DERBYSHIRE

Tales of Murder and Manslaughter
c.1700–1900

SCOTT C LOMAX

First Published in Great Britain in 2011 by
Wharncliffe Books
an imprint of
Pen and Sword Books Ltd.
47 Church Street
Barnsley
South Yorkshire
S70 2AS

Copyright © Scott C Lomax 2011

ISBN: 978-1-84884-621-0

Typeset in 11/13pt Plantin by Concept, Huddersfield.

Printed and bound in England by CPI UK.

Pen & Sword Books Ltd incorporates the Imprints of Pen
& Sword Aviation, Pen & Sword Family History, Pen &
Sword Maritime, Pen & Sword Military, Pen & Sword
Discovery, Wharncliffe Local History, Wharncliffe True
Crime, Wharncliffe Transport, Pen & Sword Select, Pen
& Sword Military Classics, Leo Cooper, The Praetorian
Press, Remember When, Seaforth Publishing and
Frontline Publishing.

For a complete list of Pen & Sword titles please contact
PEN & SWORD BOOKS LIMITED
47 Church Street
Barnsley
South Yorkshire
S70 2BR
England
E-mail: enquiries@pen-and-sword.co.uk
Website: www.pen-and-sword.co.uk

Contents

Acknowledgements

I would like to express my thanks to my Uncle, Brian Dickens, who sadly died during the writing of this book but who persuaded me to keep going at a time when I had almost abandoned the project. His words of encouragement and his great interest in crime in Derbyshire, which helped spark my own fascination with historic crimes, was a source of inspiration for this compilation.

I would also like to thank my partner for her patience, support and for accompanying me on some of the visits to various locations across Derbyshire when taking photographs. I am also grateful to the few people I encountered on my rambles who provided me with occasional snippets of local information.

Finally I would like to thank Brian Elliott and everyone at Wharncliffe and Pen and Sword Books for helping bring these old and often forgotten cases back to life.

Introduction

Murder has a fascination that has existed throughout the ages. It is an aspect of humanity which thankfully few of us have ever had to personally deal with but most of us wish to try and understand. There is now, always has been, and probably always will be, a morbid curiosity in gaining a peek into the darker side of human nature. The way in which this curiosity has manifested itself has changed over time. In the times of the cases featured in this book, trials and executions attracted large crowds. Today, whilst visitors flock in and out of courtrooms to see the accused, the media has opened up the experience to people from the comfort of their own homes. Yet the curiosity and interest is no less. If anything it is arguably more.

Murder has been a scourge of society throughout the ages. The past was as dangerous, if not more so, because people lived in a greater age of innocence where even in small communities and villages horrific murders could and did take place - as the following chapters reveal only too well. History allows us to learn from the past. The study of historic crimes, as well as satisfying curiosities and providing dark and chilling entertainment, can help improve knowledge of how and why crime was, and still is, committed.

Deadly Derbyshire is a guide to murder and manslaughter committed within the confines of the county and across the full extent of the county area during the eighteenth and nineteenth centuries. It is based on extensive searches of the newspaper archives, uncovering a large number of cases never before written about in any other published source. This compendium complements and accompanies other books published by Pen and Sword Books, including *Foul Deeds and Suspicious Deaths in and Around Chesterfield, More Foul Deeds and Suspicious Deaths in and Around Chesterfield, Unsolved Murders in and Around Derbyshire* and *Foul Deeds and Suspicious Deaths in and Around*

Derby, to produce arguably the most comprehensive series of books about Derbyshire's deadly past ever to appear in print.

Within these pages there are tales of murder and manslaughter in many of their manifestations, committed for many motivations. There are cases of murder for greed, to abate financial distress, for sex, for jealousy, for revenge, for convenience, and cases where manslaughter was committed due to mental illness at a time when psychiatric problems were barely understood by the medical community let alone the population at large. Furthermore, you will read of cases where violence erupted with fatal consequences due to alcohol, usually involving arguments over trivial matters, but which resulted in bloodshed and the loss of life.

This book contains cases of murders that shocked the entire county, with developments followed by people nationwide. There is, for example, the murder of Elizabeth Goodwin, at Wigwell Hall, near Wirksworth. Goodwin's murder was highly prominent in newspapers across the country at the time but has been barely written about since. This lamentable tragedy saw Goodwin, an upper-class niece of a well respected magistrate, killed by her rejected lover; showing that whilst the majority of murder victims were amongst the working people during the Victorian era, murder in general and murders of passion did not discriminate by social class. There is also the case of a police officer who was shot dead in Derby in the line of duty, with a trial so controversial it sparked questions in Parliament, and required the intervention of the Home Secretary.

You will also read of little-published cases, such as instances of murders and suicides, which took place in Chesterfield, Milltown near Ashover, Stoney Houghton near Pleasley and Derby. There is the story of a fatal fight over three eggs which resulted in a killer receiving a prison sentence of just two years, in 1858. Other cases include numerous children, and also some adults, who were dumped in rivers and canals and whose identities were as much a mystery as those who ended the victims' lives. Most notable is the singular case of the child who was found in the canal at Derby in 1851, resulting in one of the most controversial criminal cases of the Victorian period for Derbyshire. A fatal duel in the name of honour is recounted, as is the case of a man who murdered his wife and who found himself on the last ship to transport convicts to Australia as a consequence. And then there is the death of Mary Ann Winfield in Derby, who was found drowned. Did she fall from a bridge or was she pushed?

The less well-known cases are of equal, and occasionally arguably greater interest from a criminological point of view. The fact they have never before been written about in book form is not because of a lack of interesting points of the offences but is often because no one was brought to trial due to the suicide of the culprit or because no killer was ever identified. If a trial had commenced it is likely that these little-known crimes would have provoked as much, if not more interest among the people of Derbyshire of the time; and would have interested those of us who study historic criminal cases. Take, for example, the crimes of Elizabeth Berry, a probable serial killer who gained experience in her criminal career in Castleton, where she nearly got away with the murder of her mother. Then there are the unsolved murders of John Mayna and Enoch Stone. Mayna was murdered in Sleet Moor near Alfreton, having been robbed of a waistcoat containing a large sum of money. Stone's death caused huge shock across Sponden, resulting in a large cash reward being offered for the capture of his killer. A memorial at the spot at which he was mortally wounded still exists and a street was named in his memory.

Some of the crimes recounted here continue to be spoken of today, although most of the others have been forgotten for a century or longer. What is clear is that the following chapters will remind all of us of the dark side of Derbyshire's past. The stories of how cases were resolved prior to the dawn of modern forensic techniques, using good old-fashioned detective work, remain very interesting for us today. But in some cases deadly secrets were taken to the grave.

CHAPTER 1

The Price of Infidelity:
The Murder of Hannah Hewitt
1732

John Hewitt was a married man for whom the words 'til death us do part' came to have a more sinister meaning when his wife Hannah paid the ultimate price for her husband's adultery. Hewitt, a butcher, had an affair with the elderly landlady of The Crown public house in Nuns Green, Derby, but one affair was not enough. Whilst having liaisons with the landlady he became acquainted with her servant, Rosamund Ollerenshaw, and began a relationship with her too.

For how long the affairs existed is uncertain, although it appears they were far from short-term flings, but Hewitt and his mistresses were unwilling to allow the situation to continue. Filled with jealousy and desperate for Hewitt's undivided attention, the landlady made a poisoned pancake and had it taken to Hewitt's wife, by Ollerenshaw. Hannah seemingly did not have any suspicions as she ate the gift but she soon developed severe stomach pains and began vomiting. It was said that she repeatedly vomited the food she had consumed and that some of it was eaten by a pig which quickly became ill itself and died. Hannah also died, in agony, just three hours after eating her final meal.

Hewitt and his two mistresses stood trial for the murder at the March assizes but only Ollerenshaw and Hewitt were found guilty. The landlady was acquitted due to a lack of evidence against her, even though her role of preparing the pancake seems almost without question. Indeed, Ollerenshaw claimed she had been asked by her employer to put poison in Hannah's broth. She did as she was requested but the poison was not of a high enough quantity to do any serious harm to the butcher's wife, who probably never knew of her husband's infidelity, never mind that there was a plot to kill her.

What Hewitt's exact role was in the crime remains unclear due to a lack of available sources and scant reporting in the press. Perhaps he incited his lovers to carry out the poisoning or at least was a co-conspirator; or perhaps he added the poison to the pancake without the landlady's knowledge. But the latter seems unlikely if Ollerenshaw's story is to be believed.

Convicted of one murder, Ollerenshaw then confessed to a further homicide, of her illegitimate child, who it was speculated had been fathered by Hewitt. She described the place she had buried her infant, and bones of a child, aged perhaps about seven months, were found when the spot was excavated.

Despite the nature of the crime, and the fact that Ollerenshaw had committed two murders, there was some public sympathy for the couple. The pair were pitied and a large number of people prayed for them as they prepared to be plunged into the afterlife on 29 March. The killers were hanged in their shrouds, the grim scene watched by a large number of people.

A contemporary sketch of a public execution during the nineteenth century.
Author's collection

Eighteenth-century Murders of Unwanted Children: The Crimes of Mary Dilkes, Charles Kirkman, Susannah Moreton and James Preston 1754, 1759 and 1796

Mary Dilkes, 1754

When the body of a newborn baby was found on a sandbank, near the island in the River Derwent, just off the Station Approach in Derby, known then and today as The Holmes, during the first week of January 1754, there was understandable upset amongst the local populace. The authorities began looking for anyone who was suspected of recently giving birth. Enquiries soon found a suspect, Mary Dilkes, on 8 January, following information that she had given birth but that her child was unaccounted for.

When questioned, Dilkes admitted she had indeed given birth to the child but that another woman had delivered it and taken the baby away immediately afterwards. Dilkes claimed she did not know her child had died and she flatly denied having abandoned or killed the baby.

The authorities were not convinced by Dilkes' story and so they questioned her again on 14 January, when she again admitted she had given birth to the infant on 1 January; but this time she claimed that it had died of natural causes soon after birth and she had then disposed of it. Accepting that her original statement regarding the other woman was untruthful, those questioning the mother became convinced that the deceit had been to cover up for what they had suspected: that Mary Dilkes had wilfully ended the life of her child. She was therefore charged with infanticide and remanded into custody, in Derby Gaol.

The Holmes, a natural island in the River Derwent on which Mary Dilkes left her baby's corpse in January 1754. The author

There has been a gaol in Derby since 1588, the year that the Spanish Armada sailed into English waters. An Act of Parliament had ordered the establishment of a gaol in 1532 but it took more than half a century for that order to be followed. Prior to its construction in the Corn Market, over the Markeaton Brook which acted as the town's sewer, prisoners had been sent to Nottingham. In 1754, Dilkes would have been suffering from the cramped conditions of the old and decrepit prison, her only hope being that the court which would try her for murder would offer some leniency.

On 21 March that same year, she was found guilty of murder, after a three-hour trial before Mr Justice Birch, despite having protested her innocence. There was no leniency from Birch as he donned his black cap and ordered that Dilkes should be taken to a place of lawful execution where she should be 'hanged by the neck until she was dead'.

Two days later, prior to being executed, Dilkes made a confession to a chaplain. She was the first woman to be hanged in Derby for more than two decades and a larger than usual crowd turned out to witness this historic event; and to see justice, as they understood it, being served on the woman who was capable of killing a defenceless baby. She had prayed for some time with the chaplain at the place of execution. After hanging for the usual time, her body was taken down and dissected at the County Hall, for the benefit of medical students, and not to mention for the benefit of the public, who, in need of further entertainment after watching an execution, would try and watch the poor woman being opened up 'for study'. After dissection a corpse would often be left on display for two days to allow as many people as possible to view it.

Charles Kirkman, 1759

A large crowd was to form outside the prison five years later when it became apparent to the authorities, and those concerned with maintaining a law abiding community, that the punishment given to Mary Dilkes had not acted as a deterrent.

Just five years after Mary Dilkes killed her newborn child, another infanticide took place in Derby. On 27 February 1759, a newborn baby was found in the Gaol Brook in Derby, part of which can still be seen from Bridge Street. The mother of the

The County Court at St Mary's Street, Derby, where prisoners stood trial and where many of the county's killers were executed. The author

The Gaol Brook, Derby, in which Charles Kirkman left the body of his newly born son in 1759. The author

unfortunate child, Sarah Hall, was soon identified and taken to the magistrates for questioning, but no evidence was forthcoming to link her to the killing of the child.

After extensive questioning, Hall was released without charge, with her innocence well established in the minds of the magistrates. Charles Kirkman, her lover and the father of the child, was also arrested and, under intense questioning, his guilt became apparent. Kirkman was charged with killing his own son. He was taken to the newly-built gaol in Friar Gate, a short distance behind which the gaolbrook flowed. The prison had opened in 1756 and was large enough to hold twenty-one criminals and twenty-six debtors, but it soon became over-crowded. The cells measured 7ft by 7ft 4 inches. The gaol no longer survives, the above-ground structure was demolished to make way for Georgian houses. However, the underground prison cells were not destroyed by that development and are still accessible. One has to wonder whether Kirkman considered the presence of the gaol so close to where he stood whilst he dumped his son's body and, if he did, whether this stirred any emotions in his mind.

A contemporary sketch of the gaol in Friar Gate which houses Derby's prisoners as they awaited trial and, often, execution, between 1756 and 1827. The legal place of execution for many of Derby's killers. Author's collection

Hall told the magistrates that Kirkman had delivered the baby and agreed to testify against him at trial. Kirkman had denied any involvement in the child's birth and death but his defence was not accepted. He was therefore convicted before Mr Baron Smythe on 19 March and executed five days later, still protesting his innocence. Naturally one has to wonder, especially in light of miscarriages of justice in recent decades, whether intense questioning using eighteenth-century methods could have ever resulted in false confessions or incriminating evidence. We will never know if Kirkman, and many other convicted killers, were guilty, unless there was direct evidence proving that to be the case. As far as the justice system of the day was concerned, Charles Kirkman murdered his son and, like most killers, deserved to die.

Susan Moreton and James Preston, 1796
James Preston faced the same fate towards the end of the eighteenth century. Susannah Moreton was twenty-four years old when her baby was born, in 1796, but the young mother had no intention of bringing up the child.

Upon the birth, Moreton decided to conceal the fact she had been in labour and given birth. She hid her child in a chamber pot, where it later died. When questioned over the death, Moreton claimed the baby had been stillborn but this was not accepted and her guilt was deemed to have been proven when her co-accused, seventy-year-old James Preston, admitted the baby had been alive when he helped deliver it. If he had not made this admission they may have both escaped serious punishment. Both were charged with murder and remanded in the Friar Gate gaol, which was by this time hugely over-crowded. Three prisoners were confined in each of the tiny cells. The only improvement from the time of Kirkman's confinement was the installation of a bath (in 1774) to try and tackle the problem of deteriorating sanitary conditions, which had seen gaol fever become a serious problem, although the gaol was still not cleaned until more than a decade later; and then regulations stated it was necessary to clean the walls and floors only once a year.

In March 1796, the pair faced trial for murder before Sir Giles Rooke at the Derby Assizes. Moreton's lies resulted in her conviction for murder and she was sentenced to death. Having told the authorities the child was alive in his presence, Preston implicated himself in its death and so he too was convicted. Moreton was due to be executed on 17 March but, on the very morning she was due to be hanged alongside her co-accused, her sentence was commuted to a 'life' in prison. Preston was not so lucky, however. Despite having confessed to his crime, there was no last-minute reprieve. He was hanged and his body dissected for medical research.

CHAPTER 3

The Price of Temptation:
The Murder of Mary Vickers
1776

Matthew Cocklayne, also known as Matthew Coghlan, was an Irishman by birth. He disliked school and had often been absent for weeks on end, from the age of nine or ten. However, at the age of thirteen he joined the Army and this gave him a feeling of purpose and pride. He was discharged after completing ten years of loyal service in the 33rd Regiment, without a blemish on his record, or at least having committed no wrongs that ever came to light. His respectable record changed, however, soon after entering civilian life.

Upon leaving the Army, Cocklayne moved to Derby and married but he soon became acquainted with a George Foster, who proved to be a bad influence. The pair began a career of petty theft that would escalate to murder. 'This young man [Foster] advised me frequently to commit things repugnant to civil society. He begged me to go along with him and that I should not want for money,' Cocklayne would later say in a written confession by way of explanation for how his life went wrong. One has to wonder how much of the confessions and statements are the actual words of the accused and how much influence the authorities had in the writing of them. It seems quite unlikely that a man who was barely educated would use such phrases as 'repugnant to civil society'. Nonetheless, the statement gives some background to what occurred. No doubt his military life from such a young age had made it difficult for him to settle into a 'normal' life. Even marriage could not dissuade him from taking up a life of crime that would ultimately lead to violence, murder and his own death.

It was in 1774 that Cocklayne met a servant girl who worked for an elderly widow named Mary Vickers, who lived at Full

Street in Derby. Recent times have seen most of the historic buildings in and around Full Street replaced with a multi-storey car park and other modern developments, although the Cathedral (the church of All Saints, which became the Cathedral in 1927), the Silk Mill and The Dolphin public house are amongst few remnants of the past. Through his acquaintance with the girl, Cocklayne soon learnt that Vickers had a large sum of money in her house; a prize that was too tempting to resist even if he had any desire to resist. He also found that the widow never had more than one servant at any time. There is no evidence to suggest that the servant girl played any part in what was to follow.

Cocklayne and Foster formed their plan but their crime would not go as well as they had intended.

It was on the night of Sunday/Monday, 18/19 December 1774, that the two crooks decided to commit their wicked act. Foster had watched the house before being joined by Cocklayne after he finished work in the copper mills. When they approached the building they found the door securely locked, but that had been anticipated. The Irishman managed to climb

Full Street, Derby, where Mary Vickers lived and was brutally murdered in 1776. The author

through an unsecure window and then unlocked the door to allow Foster's entrance.

Once in the building they wasted no time. A wooden chest in Vickers' room was broken open by Cocklayne, to reveal approximately £300 (worth c.£20,000 today) contained within a number of purses. Several rings were also found and some sources say they were taken, but burglary and theft were not the only crime committed that night. If they had stopped at burglary then it is quite likely they would have successfully stolen what was a huge sum and got away with it, had they left the area; but what took place that night resulted in a determined effort to catch the two men.

Cocklayne's criminal record was now to have added to it the charge of murder and Foster was to be considered to be his accomplice, although one could easily argue that both men played almost equal roles. In order to steal what they did the two men felt that they had to restrain Vickers. However, if it was due to panic, or to ensure that the elderly, defenceless lady would be unable to later recognise the two criminals, they did far more than what was necessary for their purposes.

The men had headed upstairs and entered her room and must have woken the elderly lady, for she jumped out of bed. Foster knocked her to the ground and held her down while Cocklayne hit her with an iron bar, or 'pin' as he would later call it, fatally wounding her. According to Cocklayne's later account of events, Foster had stuffed a handkerchief in her mouth to prevent her from screaming. The ferocity of the attack meant that there was no chance the victim could have survived.

It being the festive period, and despite the late hour, a procession of musicians passed by the house, which caused great alarm in Cocklayne's mind. He panicked and decided that as soon as possible he and Foster needed to escape the building.

Killing Vickers, however, was not enough to allow the criminals to get away with the perfect crime, for Vickers was not the only person who saw the murderers. Before they had left the building a servant saw the partners in crime as they tried to make their escape, having no doubt been alerted to the situation by what would have been some considerable noise. Cocklayne threatened the servant, an action that would later lead to his guilt being proven, although if he had acted upon his threat it is likely he would have got away with murder. The pair then fled along Full Street, through the churchyard of the cathedral and on to Nuns Green. There they agreed to temporarily go their separate ways to prevent capture, believing that a hunt for the old woman's killers would rely upon the servant's evidence that two men were responsible and therefore the authorities would most likely be looking for two fugitives. Cocklayne travelled to Leek and Foster went to Liverpool via Chester. They had agreed to meet in Liverpool where they would travel by ship to Ireland. However, prior to their departure from the Liverpool docks, Cocklayne began to panic more greatly as he sat in a tavern. A wanted notice was read out to those in the tavern to inform them that a hunt was underway for two men who had committed a burglary and murder in Derby. According to Cocklayne's later account, he had not known for certain that the elderly lady had died – until he heard the wanted notice.

The murderers travelled by ship to Dublin, with renewed determination to avoid capture, but they had no intention of lying low. Instead of going into hiding the pair continued their criminal activities in Ireland. It was a career choice which saw their undoing. A period of highway robbery commenced, although, like burglary, the pair were not good at this new activity; upon holding up a chaise containing two men, Foster was shot in the head and died three days later. Cocklayne was arrested and his identity was realized. Presumably the authorities had assumed he must have been the killer due to his criminal activities in Ireland and his sudden fleeing of Derby and England after the murder. He was brought back to Derby to await his trial for the murder of Mary Vickers.

The prosecution at trial could not present an open and shut case and Cocklayne had good reason to believe he could potentially get away with murder. The servant who had seen the two men flee had not seen Cocklayne's face and because he had not been found in possession of any of the victim's belongings he was hopeful that the circumstantial case against him would lead to an acquittal. Nonetheless, the servant's evidence proved to be damning to Cocklayne's chances of gaining freedom. She may not have recognised his appearance, no doubt seeing him in the dark, but she certainly recognised his voice as being the one that told her, 'Go back upstairs or I'll take your life this minute.' This voice recognition proved to be sufficient in the minds of the members of the jury to conclude Cocklayne's guilt and the thirty-year-old was sentenced to death accordingly.

Having protested his innocence throughout his time on remand and during his trial, in the days before his execution he decided to confess that it was he who had mortally wounded Mary Vickers. He was hanged on 21 March 1776, on Nuns Green Tree, following ninety minutes of religious devotions with a Methodist preacher, in the hope of being forgiven for his wicked crimes. At the place of legal execution he secured the noose around his own neck and helped the executioner pull the cap over his face. Following his painful and prolonged death the authorities wished for his body to be dissected, as was the custom, to increase medical knowledge; but execution was insufficient punishment in the eyes of the family of the victim, who requested, as was their right, that he should be gibbeted, to make an example of the killer and deter others from following in his wicked footsteps.

A gibbet was a padlocked or riveted cage in which a corpse was placed on a post often 30ft high, spiked with nails to prevent the body from being taken down by friends or relatives of the convict. The 1752 Murder Act had regularized gibbeting as part of a sentence. At the time of Cocklayne's conviction, when a request for gibbeting was made, it was usually accepted and so Cocklayne's dead body was hanged in chains at Bradshaw Hay (believed to be near modern-day Bradshaw Way), as a deterrent to anyone with similar murderous intentions. There it remained as a grisly reminder of one of eighteenth-century Derbyshire's most violent crimes, until five years later, when a gale blew the mostly skeletal remains down, although some skin and hair was still preserved. Its presence was a most gruesome sight for a most gruesome crime.

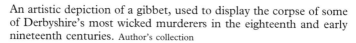

An artistic depiction of a gibbet, used to display the corpse of some of Derbyshire's most wicked murderers in the eighteenth and early nineteenth centuries. Author's collection

CHAPTER 4

A Warning From the Gallows: The Murder of John Grundy 1788

Brotherly love was not something that Thomas Grundy had much regard for. Indeed, at the Derby Assizes in March 1788 he was convicted of murdering his brother, John, who died from poisoning. Unfortunately few details survive of Grundy's crime, with reports focusing more on the sensational claims he made at the place of his execution, when he committed a further moral wrong of accusing an innocent woman of murder.

On the day chosen by the judge to be the one on which justice was to be exacted, Saturday 29 March 1788, Grundy was put in the cart at 11.30am. The twenty-year-old appeared greatly affected by the prospect of what lay ahead of him, and he had to lean against the executioner, crying bitterly throughout the journey. At the tree he prayed with the Reverend Henry. Two others then prayed with him.

After praying, he turned his attention to the crowd, some of whom will have heard his address, but his words will have been drowned by the heckling of those who only wished to see a man die and who were not interested in having to listen to a speech. Grundy informed the spectators 'in a most solemn manner', according to the press of the day, that he accepted his sentence but that his brother's wife, Mary, with whom he had become criminally connected, had accelerated the death of her father by poison and had poisoned a child. The details of this relationship are unknown but it would appear Grundy was alluding to an alleged affair. He begged the young amongst the large number of spectators to take heed and to avoid false women because it was the consequence of involving himself with such a person that he had committed the crime. He said that the stories against a Mary Warren were untrue and she was innocent. He added he had made his peace with God and was ready to die in the knowledge that he would gain salvation.

The cart was pulled away from under the condemned man, causing Grundy's body to be suspended from the gallows and he died an agonising death. After his execution Grundy's body was taken to the County Hall where he was publicly dissected on the Monday, again in front of many spectators.

As a result of Grundy's final statement at the gallows, on the Tuesday morning, Mary Grundy was questioned to determine whether there was any truth in the story. After a long examination before F N C Mundy, which was attended by approximately twenty people from Dale Abbey, many of whom were also questioned, it was found that there was no doubt she had not poisoned her father, her child or her husband.

CHAPTER 5

The Parwich Poisoner: William Webster 1807

Financial distress can cause many an otherwise sane individual to consider turning to crime. When an individual is in debt far beyond his or her means, and so much so that home and liberty are at stake, then the mind may turn to thoughts of severe action. When the demands for money become stronger then the source of those demands can often find themselves becoming the target of threats, violence and, occasionally, death.

This rule of criminal history was the reason for one of Derbyshire's most infamous poisoning cases in which, only by chance, did only two people die in what could quite conceivably have been an act of mass murder.

By the beginning of 1807, William Webster owed several hundred pounds to a man named Thomas Dakin, in whose home he lodged at Parwich, a small village six miles north of Ashbourne. Webster knew he had no means of ever being able to pay those debts and it was a most naïve action on Dakin's part to have lent the man so much money. Recognising his inability to honour his debts, he resorted to the usual initial tactic of trying to buy time. When questions were asked about why the money was not being repaid, Webster forged letters from people who claimed to owe him money. He then forwarded these to Dakin, saying that once he received the money from these individuals, none of whom actually owed him any money, then he would be able to pay Dakin what he was due. By pretending he would be able to pay his debts in the long term, Webster was therefore able to temporarily delay his problems, but a more permanent solution was necessary.

By 11 February, Webster realised that the forged notes would not be enough to extract himself from his situation and that he would be unable to pay what he owed no matter how hard he worked. If he had committed any minor offences such as theft, and there is no evidence that he did commit any such offences, other than forgery, no amount of effort would have been able to pay back the borrowed money. Rather than face a term in a debtors' prison, and all that that entailed, Webster instead chose to take a gamble and commit the crime of murder. It was to cost two totally innocent individuals, neither of whom had any direct association to the debt that was owed.

For how long he had contemplated, and prepared to commit murder, is uncertain, but on that February day Webster decided to drink with Dakin in an inn owned by John Sims. There, Webster mixed what was only ever described as being a 'corrosive sublimate' into Dakin's ale, but the inexperienced poisoner overdid it. This is a common mistake made by those who try to kill by this popular method of murder, and it usually takes several attempts of trial and error before the correct, effective dose of poison is successfully administered. Upon tasting his drink, Dakin was soon overcome with a nauseous feeling and refused to drink any more of his ale. Thus he did not consume sufficient poison to do anything more than provide temporary sickness.

Undeterred, at breakfast the following day the landlord was given a hot milk drink with wine or spice. Little did he know that his posset, as the drink was known, would contain another dose of a more lethal chemical: arsenic. Unanticipated by Webster, the rest of the family were also to have this drink. Again the poisoner failed; there was too little arsenic and so the family were briefly ill but soon recovered. Despite two incidents having occurred in Webster's presence, there was seemingly no suspicion aroused against the lodger. No doubt the family suspected there was a problem with the water, something that was very common in the early nineteenth century, when there was little or no access to clean water for the majority of people.

Gaining experience through his failures, Webster tried his murderous plot again, believing he would be successful on his third attempt. This time he put arsenic in the teapot and in doing so he must have realised that not only Thomas Dakin would be affected. Dakin drank the tea and became ill, much more seriously than on the previous two attempts on his life. The four Dakin children and their servant Jane Fearn all suffered serious illness but made full recoveries, as did Dakin. This was more than what can be said for Dakin's wife Elizabeth and her sister Mary Roe, both of whom suffered the violent stomach cramps, sickness and other symptoms associated with arsenic poisoning. After an agonising and lengthy period of suffering, both sisters lost their lives.

A lack of knowledge and a trusting nature may have prevented Dakin and his household from realising that the three poison attempts were suspicious, but the authorities and trained doctors were not so easily fooled.

It was soon determined that poison was responsible for the deaths and near deaths and the finger of suspicion inevitably pointed to the only individual in the household who had not suffered any illness, despite him having been present on all three occasions when the ill effects of the drinks were experienced. Webster was arrested, charged and indicted with the murders of Mrs Dakin and Mrs Roe, by poisoning. He was also charged with the attempted murders of Tom Dakin, Jane Fearn and the four children. He denied any responsibility.

On 20 March 1807, Dakin was convicted, following an eleven-hour trial, during which he protested his innocence throughout. His protestations were short-lived, however. As was often the case, faced with the knowledge that he would pay the ultimate price for his crimes regardless of what he said, he confessed immediately prior to his execution in the hope of gaining a place in heaven. He was hanged six days after his conviction.

CHAPTER 6

Commit No Crime:
The Murder of Hannah Oliver
1815

The prospect of starting a family, and the financial pressures associated with the arrival of a baby, especially in families in abject poverty, can and has resulted in the full range of crimes over the course of the history of civilisation. Of course, the extreme end of the range is murder and it was this crime which befell Hannah Oliver in 1815.

Hannah Oliver was a seventy-year-old toll-keeper at the Wardlow Mires turnpike, one of the main roads to Stoney Middleton and Bakewell, one or two miles north of Litton. It was a cottage at this location, in which Oliver lived, which her killer broke into on 15 January.

The villain seemingly had no intention of committing only burglary, probably because if he allowed the elderly woman to live then he would be recognised, being a local man. Oliver tried to struggle with her attacker but was overcome by his greater strength. He strangled the poor woman with her own silk scarf, before taking the toll money, any other money he could find; and also stole a pair of red leather shoes. In one of those extremely strange coincidences, it is said that on that very same night Oliver's sister, who was also a toll-keeper on the Yorkshire Moors, was also murdered.

When morning broke, the blowing of the stagecoach warning bugles failed to attract attention. A barmaid of the local inn, the Devonshire Arms (now the Three Stags' Heads Inn) heard the bugles and went to investigate. Oliver's body was found lying in the doorway of the cottage. It was clear she had been murdered.

The attention of the authorities was quickly directed at a local man named Anthony Lingard who was twenty-one years old. Lingard had got his girlfriend pregnant and knew that he could not afford to bring up a child. Indeed, he did not wish to bring up the child but instead buy the woman's silence. Crime ran in the Lingard family; his brother had been a highwayman and had been transported to Australia. Lingard took inspiration from his sibling but committed a crime of far greater gravity. The need for money drove him to commit murder, and he thought his pregnant lover might like the shoes, so he stole them to provide a parting gift. The shoes, however, would lead to his downfall.

The mother of his child did not like the shoes and became suspicious about how Lingard had obtained them. He insisted he had bought them, and then claimed he had exchanged them for a pair of stockings, although admitting that they had been stolen. Dissatisfied with this response, her suspicions grew. Unable to persuade her to take the money and shoes, Lingard hid them in a haystack and then later removed them to his own home, but his girlfriend soon reported her suspicions to the authorities.

Following a search by the constable, during which the shoes were recovered, a local cobbler from Stoney Middleton, by the name of Samuel Marsden, confirmed he had made the shoes and that they had been made for Hannah Oliver. A deeply religious man, Marsden had always included a small piece of paper with a religious motto or text from the Bible within the make up of the shoes. The shoes found at Lingard's home were taken apart and the ironic words 'Commit no crime' were found within them. There was no direct evidence, however, linking Lingard to the crime. In fact it was only his possession of the shoes, and his inability to satisfactorily account for how he obtained them, that was seen to be proof of his guilt. The possession of an item of clothing stolen from a murder scene does not in itself prove culpability of that murder and so Lingard hoped he would get away with his crime. The suspicions of his girlfriend were not based on any evidential grounds and so she was not considered to be able to offer anything that would greatly contribute to a conviction. However, it was argued that with him having tried to give his girlfriend the shoes, so soon after the murder, there was no time to have bought them or exchanged them with any other individual and he was never able to offer any account of whom he obtained them from.

Despite the highly circumstantial nature of the evidence against him, and despite the defence's best efforts at trial, Lingard was convicted of the murder, on 8 March 1815, following only a few minutes of deliberations by the jury, and the verdict has always been considered to be correct. He protested his innocence to the end.

The judge, Sir John Bayley, sentenced Lingard to death, a punishment carried out on 28 March, but the public outrage surrounding the crime was so great that the judge requested that an example should be made of this murderer. And so, a few days after his execution, on 1 April, Lingard's corpse was suspended in a gibbet at Wardlow Mires where his body remained in the chains, covered in a canvas and tar, to act as a deterrent against anyone who intended to commit murder. The grim spectre did not work. In 1818, the teenage murderess Hannah Bocking planned to poison her victim, Jane Grant, a crime committed with the skeletal remains within the gibbet in full view. The gibbet remained in situ until 10 April 1826, a total of eleven years, before being dismantled. Lingard's remains were buried on the site at which they had previously been displayed. The name Gibbet Field is a lasting reminder of its macabre past.

Almost as macabre as having a corpse on display, was that when a fair was held in Litton, Lingard's remains were taken there. Lots of entertainment was provided and there were traders' stalls with souvenirs on sale. Such was the level of morbidity that surrounded crime and punishment in days gone by.

Yet another form of entertainment was associated with Lingard's death and gibbeting. A poem, written by William Newton, was said to be based on the thoughts of Lingard's father. It was entitled '*The supposed soliloquy of the father under the gibbet of his son, upon one of the Peak Mountains near Wardlow.*' Part of it reads:

> *Art thou my son suspended here on high*
> *Ah what a sight to meet a father's eye*
> *To see what most I prized, what most I loved,*

What most I cherished, and once approved,
Hung in mid air to feed the nauseous worm,
And waving horrid in the midnight storm!

This poem raised awareness of what had for a while been regarded as a barbaric practice that served no purpose other than to frighten children and blight the landscape with corpses. Its verses did help bring an end to the use of gibbeting and, indeed, Anthony Lingard was the last man to be gibbeted in Derbyshire. The 'odious practice' came to an end in 1834.

CHAPTER 7

A Lucky Killer:
Elizabeth Jones
1817

Previous pages have recounted the stories of parents killing their offspring. It has sadly been a familiar tale over the centuries, but the murder perpetrated by Elizabeth Jones, although similar in many regards, was entirely different in terms of the outcome for the killer.

It was in Duffield, a small town between Derby and Belper, on 7 November 1817, that tragedy fell upon Jones' five-month-old child. That day, Jones was travelling to Derby from Birmingham, with two of her eight children, after being

The Derbyshire town in which Elizabeth Jones killed her youngest child in 1817. Later, the town in which Edward Marsh drank before his unexplained death in 1854. The author

abandoned by the father. She knew that the father had gone to Derby so she decided to follow him. The abandonment must have played heavy on her mind, with eight children in need of support, but that in no way justified what followed.

Jones got as far as Duffield and there she killed the youngest of the two children, no doubt in a state of depression, desperation and anguish. Her desired medium of causing death was suffocation and it was this means which she applied in her task. She pushed straw on top of the young boy, whose age is not recorded, in a barn, and sat on him until it was clear that he was dead. The body was then hidden between two hayricks.

With such a poor attempt of disposing of the body, Jones' crime was soon discovered. Her guilt was also quickly established when she confessed to her crime. The verdict at the inquest was that she was guilty of wilful murder. Jones spent five months on remand in the increasingly overcrowded Friar Gate gaol, before charges against her were remarkably dropped and she walked free. Unfortunately the reasons for this dramatic turn of events are not recorded. It goes without saying that she was more fortunate than her contemporaries who would have expected, at the very least, a lengthy period of imprisonment if found guilty of even the lesser charge of manslaughter on the grounds of insanity. What became of Jones and her remaining children is unknown.

CHAPTER 8

A Fatal Duel: The Murder of Dr William Cuddie 1821

Doctors are well advised to keep relations with their patients strictly professional. If Dr William Cuddie had followed this code he might have missed the opportunity to spend personal time with the woman who would become the love of his life; but it would have prevented the tragic duel that cost him his life.

For some reason there has been a certain amount of romanticism surrounding the portrayal of duels, with images of them being carried out between members of the upper classes to settle family scores, in the name of family honour, or to satisfy the grievance of an individual who felt he and his family had been insulted. There is, and never has been, any honour in killing and, certainly in Georgian England, those responsible for fatal duels were regarded as no less a criminal than any other individual who maliciously ended a life.

Cuddie, a thirty-one-year-old Scotsman, was a former naval surgeon who had moved to Winster, a rural village located five miles from Matlock, four years before his death. There he met Miss Mary Brittlebank, the daughter of an eminent local solicitor. As she was in poor health he regularly saw her in his capacity as a doctor, but the professional relationship quickly developed a romantic dimension. Her family disapproved of the liaison and made their hostility and increasing anger known to the surgeon. On Monday 21 May 1821, the couple were walking together until Mary's brother, William, approached and demanded she leave with him, having exchanged fierce words with the surgeon. William Brittlebank was angered by what he considered to be improper language, so much so that he sent a challenge for a duel that evening. In a note, William wrote:

> Sir, I expect satisfaction for the insult you dared to offer me at a time when you knew that my situation with a helpless woman prevented my chastising you. Name your time and place, the bearer will wait for an answer.
>
> Yours, William Brittlebank, Junior.
>
> I shall be attended by a friend and prepared with pistols, and if you don't meet I shall post you as a coward.

Cuddie failed to respond, but Brittlebank was not content with only posting Cuddie as a coward, so a second challenge was sent in a note the following morning, 22 May. Upon receiving the note the messenger was told by Cuddie that he would not respond to the challenge and would not meet the challenger. A mutual friend, Mr Spencer, a surgeon from Bakewell, was called for by William Brittlebank. Brittlebank and his brother Francis were accompanied by Spencer to Cuddie's home, joined en route by Andrew Brittlebank. Spencer entered the house and informed Cuddie that he must either make an apology or prepare for a duel. Cuddie refused to do either.

However, eventually pistols were provided for both men by Spencer, on the gravel of Cuddie's garden outside the Bank House. They paced fifteen yards and, upon being given a signal, turned and fired. Cuddie sustained a shot, the bullet becoming lodged in his bowels, and he died in agony at 1pm the following day. It was thought that Cuddie had fired a shot but had missed, although some speculated that Cuddie's pistol had not been loaded.

At the inquest the jury returned verdicts of wilful murder against the Brittlebank brothers and Mr Spencer, based largely upon a death-bed declaration made by Cuddie, on 22 May, to Philip Gell, a Justice of the Peace. Francis and Andrew Brittlebank were tried for murder on 14 August 1821, but were both acquitted. William, meanwhile, had escaped, despite there being a £100 reward for his capture. He was last seen in Manchester on 24 May and was understood to have then fled to

Australia, from where he never returned. Cuddie's killers had got away with murder.

One has to wonder whether, if Cuddie's firearm had been loaded and he had been lucky to pull the trigger a fraction of a second quicker than his opponent with a shot on target, killing Brittlebank, what punishment would he have received, given that he was coerced into taking part in the duel? As it happened he paid the ultimate price for offending a man who believed his family's reputation and honour was worth defending with murder.

CHAPTER 9

An Unmotherly Instinct:
The Case of Hannah Halley
1822

There can be few types of murder more heart-rending than those committed by a mother against her young or even newborn child. The strains and stresses of a new arrival, especially for young, unmarried and unsupported women, have resulted in countless examples of such cases being included in the annals of criminal history, some of which have already been recounted. In a later chapter you will read of the tragic case of Mary Wright, but an older and particularly more barbaric example of infanticide is that which was perpetrated by Hannah Halley, bearing similarities to that of Susannah Moreton and James Preston, quarter of a century earlier.

In August 1821, Hannah Halley, aged thirty-one, was living in a lodging house on Brook Street, in Derby, which now runs off the A52 St Alkmund's Way stretch of the inner ring road on the edge of the city centre. She worked in a cotton mill at Darley Abbey. It was on the morning of 14 August that Halley's landlady and another woman noticed something was wrong with the lodger. As she walked through one of the lower rooms, they remarked upon how ill she looked. 'I am,' Halley replied, confirming that there was something wrong with her, before heading to her own room. A short time later the sound of a crying baby was heard and the two women went to investigate.

Upon entering the room it was clear to both women that Halley had just given birth to a child, which was nowhere to be seen. Halley denied this, but suspicions were increased when she was seen trying to conceal a jug under her bedding. Unconvinced by the lodger's protestations that the women had not heard any child, one of them threatened to fetch a constable and left to do so. Alarmed, Halley followed to try and prevent this action from being carried out, at which point the other woman seized upon the opportunity to examine the jug and recoiled in horror by what she saw.

Upon removing a cloth which covered the mouth of the jug, the fellow lodger saw the badly scalded body of a new-born baby. It was clear that boiling water had been poured on the infant, rendering it scalded, after it had been pushed into the jug. Remarkably, the child was still alive, but sadly passed away a few days later, on Saturday 18 August.

Halley was arrested that day and charged with murder. During her time in prison, awaiting trial, she was described as being a well-behaved prisoner who clung on to the hope that she would be acquitted of murder and would walk free from court to continue her life. The gaol was overcrowded to the point that a new prison was desperately needed. In the same year that Halley was convicted, six acres of land near Uttoxeter Road were bought to house a new gaol, which opened in 1827, its frontage still surviving at Vernon Gate. This new establishment had 164 cells to house the county's criminals.

The frontage of the gaol on Vernon Gate which housed prisoners from 1827 and was the scene of several executions of Derby's killers. The author

At her trial, before Mr Justice Best, Halley's defence put forward the argument that their client had not committed murder, but that instead she believed she had been under the influence of the Devil, who forced her to end her child's life in such a cruel manner.

The two women who heard the baby cry, the constable who attended the scene and a doctor, gave evidence against the prisoner. Their testimonies were of such strength that her conviction was inevitable. The fact that the child was heard to cry was proof it had been alive, and therefore could not have been stillborn, which proved it had been unlawfully killed. It was therefore not only a concealment of birth but an act of murder. Halley's only hope of survival, but with a lengthy term of imprisonment, was a plea of insanity and that is where the claim of the Devil's involvement came in.

The court heard that Halley had denied being with child for much of her pregnancy. She had married a man seven weeks before her child's birth, and naïvely hoped that he could be persuaded the child was his. He was not aware of his new wife's condition and was not the father of the child. On the day prior to going into labour she admitted to those with whom she had lodged that she was pregnant, but only by three months. Deceit was thus a fact and it was argued that such deception could have only been for malicious intent and that intent could only have been present in a sane person who was aware of what she was doing and who was not suffering from insanity.

The intent to commit murder of the infant was allegedly proved by the fact she denied being pregnant to such an advanced stage. She must have known she was heavily pregnant, it was argued at trial, because she had given birth to another child five years earlier. What became of that child is unknown. Denial of an impending birth, and denial of pregnancy until the day prior to birth, is not at all an indicator of an intention to kill the child upon it being born, and it was quite wrong that the jury were told otherwise. Indeed it might have been that she did not know what to do, perhaps for example considering to abandon the child, and only began to contemplate murder once the child had been born and was crying in her arms, which must have been a time of desperation that few of us can ever appreciate. Her marriage, her livelihood, her financial security would have

A particular account of the Execution of Hannah Halley, at Derby, on Monday last, March, 26, 1822, for the inhuman Murder of her own new-born infant, by crushing it into a jug, and pouring boiling water on it, with her reasons for comitting the barbarous act.

Extracted from the London Courier of the 29th March 1822.

LAST Friday, (22d instant,) Hannah Halley was tried before Mr Justice Best for the wilful murder of her infant child, in the month of August last. The evidence adduced in support of this accusation was conclusive, not merely as to the fact, but also the intention.

She was residing in lodgings at a house in Brook-Street in th's town, and about a quarter before nine in the morning of Tuesday, August 14th, passed thro' the lower room or house place, where her landlady and another female were sitting. They observed to her that she seemed very poorly, to which she replied, ' I am,' and went up stairs to her own apartment. Soon after this the cry of a child was heard by the women of the house, and on going into the prisoner's room, appearances warranted them in charging her with being just delivered. She denied the imputation with great confidence, but was observed to put under the bed a jug, which she had previously been anxious to conceal under her clothes. As she persisted in denying that a child had been born, one of the women threatened to fetch a constable to apprehend her if she did not give up the babe. This threat being repeated, and the woman actually leaving the room for the purpose she had stated, the prisoner rose from the bed on which she was sitting, and followed her to the top of the stairs. The other female took that opportunity cf drawing the jug from under the bed, and on removing a coarse cloth with which it was covered, found within it a new-born child. On examining the infant it was perceived to be dreadfully scalded, and in such a manner as to produce the conviction, that boiling water had been poured upon it after it had been thrust into the jug. Notwithstanding this treatment the child lived till the following Saturday, the 18th of August, when it died in consequence of the injury inflicted upon it by its unnatural mother. That it was her intention to destroy the infant was inferred from her constant denial of her pregnancy, (except on the day prior to her delivery, when she admitted that she was three months advanced. She could not plead ignorance of her real situation as she had born a child five years ag 3 ; but she had allowed herself to marry only about seven weeks before her delivery to a man who knew not her condition, and who was not the father of the child she meditated to destroy.

During her long imprisonment she conducted herself with propriety, but much of her behaviour must be referred to the hope, which she indulged to the very day of her trial, that she should escape. To this feeling also must be traced the solemn asseverations of her innocence made when the Judge was about to pass upon her the dreadful sentence of the law. All hope ot impunity, however, being cut off she hastened to relieve her overburdened mind by a full confession of her guilty purpose, and of the means by which she intended to carry it into effect, thus confirming the evidence adduced against her on her trial in its full extent.

The brief interval between her sentence and execution, she passed chiefly in devotional exercises with the worthy Chaplain of the Goal, and a Minister of the religious denomination to which she had formally attached herself; in taking leave of her friends, and in mental preparation for the awful scene which lay before her. She slept little, from the time of her condemnation, but had about three hours repose on the night of sunday last. Her frame was feeble, and acted upon as it had been by the consciousness of her situation, when the time arrived for her execution, she was weak and pale and powerless. Still she ascended the steps which led to the fatal platform with more firmness than was anticipated, and was brought out upon the drop she behaved with becoming fortitude. After the usual time spent in prayer, in which she joined the chaplain with apparent devotion, the platform fell, and she died with scarcely a struggle.

Hannah Halley was 31 years of age, and was a native of Mayfield in Staffordshire. At the time of her marriage and of her committing the crime for which she has paid the forfeiture of life, she was living in Derby, and worked at the cotton-mill Darley. After hanging the usual time, the body was taken down and given to the surgeons for dissection.

A short paper, known as a broadside, sold to those interested in the execution of Hannah Halley in 1822. Author's collection

all been jeopardised. The concept of post-natal depression and related illnesses are reasonably well understood and accepted today, but two centuries ago this was not the case. Any ill state of mind, if Halley was suffering from such a disorder, does not, of course, in any way excuse the cruel act of inhumanity that resulted in the baby's death in immense pain and suffering but the simple fact is that there was no evidence at all at trial that the baby's death was premeditated.

Following her conviction, an eventual confession did state she acted with intention to kill, but there was no confession that such an intention had existed prior to the child's birth. She had committed murder but the level of premeditation remained a mystery.

Upon being convicted, Halley was taken back to Friar Gate prison and spent the weekend in a basement cell awaiting execution. During this time she turned to God in the hope of gaining comfort in the thought of salvation. She spent much of her remaining time with the prison chaplain and a minister. Friends visited and for the remainder of her life she prepared herself to die in the name of justice. On the eve of her execution, Halley slept badly, with only three hours of rest. On 22 March, as she ascended the scaffold and approached the rope which would be used to hang her, she appeared feeble, weak and pale and struggled to commence her final prayer. When the hanging took place she barely struggled and soon died.

After hanging for the usual time, the body was taken down and given to the surgeons for dissection, a practice which was coming to an end in its use of executed prisoners. Hannah Halley was the last hanged woman in Derbyshire whose body was dissected 'for medical science'.

CHAPTER 10

An Act of Drunken Wickedness: Murder and Suicide in Chesterfield 1833

An act of drunken wickedness cost two lives and nearly claimed a third, on Saturday 28 December 1833, in Chesterfield. A man named Joseph Whittaker for long had built up a reputation for ill treating his wife, although naturally at such a time little would have been done to challenge his behaviour, because what happened between a husband and wife was usually overlooked, except when a crime deemed serious by the authorities was committed. This was, after all, only a few years after the formation of the Metropolitan Police Force and forces outside of the capital were still based on the old-fashioned system of policing.

Whittaker was a tailor by trade, living on St Mary's Gate in the town, close to the famous crooked spire church of St Mary's and All Saints. Whittaker employed a fifteen-year-old apprentice named Samuel Kirk, who lived with Whittaker and his wife, Sarah, to whom he had been married for approximately one year. The couple had a child aged about six months.

The tailor went out drinking at about 4pm and arrived home at some unknown time after Kirk had retired for the night, at 10pm. Upon Whittaker's return home, after a heavy drinking session, there was a major argument in the couple's bedroom, but the topic of the heated row could not be ascertained. Whittaker closed Kirk's door and his own door, so that the row could not be heard, although the apprentice heard shouting but thought little of it at the time. He had no doubt become accustomed to such quarrels, which were a frequent occurrence.

St Mary's Gate, Chesterfield, where Joseph Whittaker murdered his wife, attempted to murder his son and committed suicide in 1833. The author

Yet the shouting ought to have raised his concerns because he later recalled his mistress having screamed, 'Sam! Sam! He has got a knife to cut my throat!' They were the only few words that were loud enough for him to distinguish what was said, and shortly afterwards there was silence.

It was only the following day that Kirk's suspicions were roused during the morning when he did not see his master and mistress, but he realised they occasionally rose late and did not give the matter too much thought. He had once tried to speak to them late one morning when they were still in bed, and had been rebuked for doing so. He did not wish to make a similar mistake. After lighting the fire he rested for the day, having no work to do. At 2pm they had still not come downstairs and so Kirk made himself some oatmeal for lunch, it being the only food he could use. However, when his master and mistress had failed to make an appearance by the evening, he became concerned, especially given that he had heard the baby moaning upon listening very carefully but that no other noise had been audible from the bedroom. At 7pm he finally went to his father's house to seek help. It would seem he had not looked inside the bedroom.

Accompanied by his father, who was called Richard, and Whittaker's brother, named Thomas, the young apprentice returned to the house half an hour after raising the alarm. They entered and Thomas shouted up from the bottom of the stairs in the hope of gaining the couple's attention. Receiving no response, with a lit candle they ascended the stairs and Thomas partly opened the bedroom door, shouting his brother's name. Again he received no reply and so he opened the door fully. Moments later, his two companions heard an exclamation of 'They are both corpses!' Both man and wife lay in bed, dead. Whittaker's throat was cut and so was his wife's, her wound extending from ear to ear. The wife's expression was described as 'placid' and it seemed she had not given much, if any, of a struggle. Whittaker had, according to the description later given, an expression 'of the most fiendish passion'. The infant was laid between them, resting on one of its mother's arms, almost dead, having also had its throat cut. The baby was taken to Richard Kirk's house, where it repeatedly vomited blood. Remarkably, it survived at least a few days despite its horrific ordeal, although there is no record as to whether it lived beyond the duration of the inquest, at which point in time its health was described as 'reasonable'.

It was concluded that Whittaker had killed his wife, attempted to kill his child and, perhaps thinking the injuries he had inflicted on the infant would be sufficient to render death, before committing suicide. Whether he had originally intended to kill the family and himself, or if he only ended his own life when overcome with remorse, or the belief he would hang for what he had done, and how much influence alcohol played, will never be known. The inquest, held at the Anchor Inn, on St Mary's Gate, on Monday 30 December. The verdict was that 'the deceased, Joseph Whittaker, had wilfully murdered his wife and cut his own throat, he being at the time of sane mind.'

Following the inquest, both Joseph and Sarah Whittaker were buried, without funeral rights. Sarah was buried on the Monday afternoon and her killer was interred under the cover of darkness on the same evening.

CHAPTER 11

The Murder of Fagan
1838

nfortunately few details could be uncovered for this, one of the most remarkable of cases. A man's refusal to join a trade union was thought to be the reason behind one of Derbyshire's most vicious murders, on Halloween night, 1838.

It was in the small town of Glossop, within the High Peak and only fifteen miles east of Manchester, on 31 October 1838, that the awful crime was discovered by a labourer, who found the body. A note found in the man's clothing suggested the victim was from Ireland and was named Fagan. A police constable was able to recognise the deceased as being the same person who had earlier applied to him for relief, having only four and a half pence to his name. The dead man had told the constable that he was a lodger who had recently begun working in the area but was forced to quit his job and so required relief.

The reason he had had to give up his job, the constable had been told, was because the Bricklayers' Trade Union had threatened to take his life if he did not join them, he had alleged. He had refused to join the union.

Perhaps this was the reason why his throat was cut from ear to ear, with a large stone weighing approximately four pounds having been used to batter the man's head repeatedly, leaving his brain 'sprinkled around' according to those who saw the sickening scene of the crime. The stone had hair, blood and brain matter adhered to it and there was no doubt it had been used as the murder weapon. The stone had caused a fracture over both eyes and the back of the man's head had been completely battered in.

James Shepherd, a constable, detained a suspect, but sadly there are no further records regarding this case that could be obtained; certainly there were no convictions and the murder of Fagan remained unsolved.

CHAPTER 12

Murder and Suicide in Milltown 1841

 double horror left a daughter devastated in the village of Milltown, near Ashover, in June 1841.

When Harriet Towndrow approached her parents' house she found the door to be locked. This was unusual, she thought, and so she looked through the window to see if anyone was at home, and was shocked to see that the contents of the house had been disturbed, with chairs knocked over. She also noted that breakfast was still on the table, having not been eaten, but she could see no sign of her parents. With great concern she approached a neighbour, John Cotes, who happened to be passing, and urged him to break open the door. This he did and a gruesome scene greeted him upon his entry.

Both John Towndrow and his wife, who were both aged about sixty years old and had several grown up children, were lying dead on the floor of the kitchen. Both had had their throats cut, with Mrs Towndrow's head having almost been severed. She also had additional injuries including one of her eyes having been destroyed, and she had several head injuries, all inflicted by a hammer. One of her hands was also bruised, which suggested she had tried to defend herself from the hammer blows.

There were no witnesses to the awful events and the nearest neighbour lived approximately fifty yards away, but heard nothing. However, it was quickly determined that this was a case of a murder and a suicide. John had beaten his wife before slashing her throat. He had then taken his own life.

The couple had argued greatly in the weeks preceding the tragedy and, as in many cases of murder, the cause of those arguments had been money. Mrs Towndrow had inherited £100 (c.£4,100 today) from a deceased relative but had refused to give the money to her husband, who was a farmer. It was believed that the growing tensions between man and wife stemmed from this refusal and had been the reason for such devastation.

The jury at the inquest recorded that John Towndrow had experienced 'temporary insanity', causing him to commit murder and suicide. Inheritance from one death had resulted in a further two, all because greed had caused homicidal mania.

CHAPTER 13

The Murders by
Thomas Cross
1847

he tragic death of Ann Cross is one which featured in the book *Foul Deeds and Suspicious Deaths in and Around Derby* by Kevin Turton. However, an important fact was not presented, presumably because the relevant incident took place some days after the frenzied stabbing attacks perpetrated by Cross' husband, Thomas; and so it was not referred to in the original coverage of the crime. Whilst researching cases through the newspaper archives it became apparent that the attack on 2 February 1847 resulted in the loss of not one, but two lives. As such, this chapter will provide only a summary of the full facts, most of the relevant parts of which are well described in Turton's book (although some additional detail will be provided relating to Ann Cross' death), but which will contribute to a fuller picture of the awful tragedy which took place on that February afternoon.

Thomas Cross had been married to Ann for twenty-three years when he decided to kill her at their well-furnished home off St Peter's Street in Derby, now in the heart of the city centre, between St Peter's church and the Westfield Shopping Centre. The couple had two children: Matilda, who was aged twenty-one, and Louisa, seventeen. On the fateful day, the two daughters were at work and Cross (employed as a gardener) and his wife were alone in the house.

Cross's activities on the morning and early afternoon of 2 February are unknown, although it's likely he spent some of this time considering his wife's death. At 2.30pm that day, Cross entered the kitchen, removed a knife and headed to the bedroom, where he found Ann was resting on the bed. It was believed she was asleep when the attack began but she did awake.

St Peter's Street, Derby, where Thomas Cross murdered his wife and mortally wounded Mrs Osborne in 1847. The author

Cries for help had been heard by neighbours, although no effort was made to assist the terror-stricken woman who had no chance against her husband, which says a lot about society in early Victorian England where desperate cries in the afternoon could simply be ignored. In a time when a level of violence by a husband to his wife was deemed acceptable perhaps such cries were fairly commonplace. Even if her cries for assistance had been answered, the crime had been completed with such swiftness that death could not have been averted. As it was, the only person who saw anything of relevance was a twelve-year-old boy who worked in a bakery and confectionary shop nearby; who happened to see Cross pacing around the bedroom immediately after the murder, but had no suspicions. Having killed his wife, Cross had washed his hands in the kitchen, one of his hands having been badly wounded during the attack.

There were no concerns or suspicions until the couple's daughter Louisa returned home from work. Upon entering the house there was nothing out of place and she made herself something to eat unaware of the horror which had taken place upstairs. Eventually, Louisa was joined by her father who also had something to eat. Nothing in what he said or how he acted gave any cause for concern but, having made food, Louisa questioned why her mother had not come downstairs to eat also. Ann's killer replied that she was ill and was resting in bed.

Worried about her mother's health, Louisa told her father that she would go and see to her and made her way to the bottom of the stairs. Unwilling to allow his daughter to see the consequences of his actions, Cross grabbed Louisa by the arm, pushed her away and blocked the entrance to the stairway. After a brief struggle, Louisa gave up her efforts and went for help, fearing that all was not well. It is not clear whether Cross had a history of violence, although the evidence suggests he did not have a particularly violent personality, and so it is unknown whether or not Louisa would have quickly suspected her mother had come to any harm at the hands of her father. Perhaps she believed Ann was, as her father had said, very ill and wanted to get help. Quite likely though she will have seen the wound on Cross's hand and begun to fear some aggressive behaviour may have taken place. She would soon discover the horrifying reality.

It was with Mrs Osborne, the wife of the owner of the bakery and confectionary shop, with whom Louisa returned. Osborne forced her way past Cross, pushing him out of the way, and Louisa rushed upstairs where she saw the consequences of her father's brutality.

Ann Cross laid on the bed in a pool of blood. It was evident to the shocked teenager that her mother's throat had been viciously slashed, a fact later confirmed as the cause of death. Her right hand had been badly cut and there was a severe wound to the wrist indicating that, in addition to having screamed for help, she had made some effort to fight for her life, attempting to disarm her husband by grabbing the blade of the knife.

It was later established she had walked around the bed briefly, quickly losing large quantities of blood, before losing consciousness and slumping on the bed, dying quickly. There was another wound under Ann's chin which was discovered later, during the post mortem.

Whilst Louisa was trying to make some initial sense of what had happened, Cross was committing another savage attack, this time on Osborne. Hearing commotion downstairs, Louisa ran down and saw her father stabbing their neighbour. Louisa intervened and grabbed the knife and was assisted by another young employee of the bakery and confectionary shop who had heard screaming. They were too late, however, Osborne having already been stabbed in the neck and face. Cross was forced to the ground and held there whilst the police were sent for. However, at about 5pm he managed to escape the hold of his captors and fled the house. He was, nonetheless, soon arrested and taken into custody. It would not have been an easy task for a man, who must surely have been covered in large amounts of blood, to have travelled far, even as darkness began to fall on Derby.

When the police examined the scene they saw two knives in the bedroom, where they lay by the side of a teaboard opposite the fire. One of the knives was a 'clamp knife' and was covered in blood.

Despite her injuries, Mrs Osborne had managed to stagger home and Mr Harewood, Mr Wood (a surgeon), Mr Fearn and Dr Ferguson later arrived to offer medical assistance. The injury was extremely serious and it was expected she would die very quickly, but Mr Fearn believed that by tying the carotid artery, which had been entirely severed, there was a chance of survival. By doing so he reduced the loss of blood and Osborne was quickly taken to the infirmary where she was able to give some basic details of the attack against her.

Great praise was given in the press to Mr Fearn, the surgeon, who had treated Osbourne. Against the odds she had survived the vicious attack. It was reported that never before had the operation been carried out successfully. In the days following the attack upon her, the *Derby Mercury* reported that she had shown signs of an improved condition and was described as being in a 'tranquil and satisfactory state'. She was conscious and had been able to eat.

The tranquil and satisfactory state did not last, however. Unfortunately, despite hopes that Osborne would make an almost full recovery, she died. One of the wounds to her neck had pierced the internal carotid artery and, although this was in the process of healing, she had been affected by a violent cough, which had caused damage to the healing wound and ultimately killed her.

Ann Cross was not committing adultery and neither was her killer. There was no evidence of any great financial problems and indeed the couple had lived in a well-furnished property which was above the level of comfort typical of members of the working class. Cross was not drunk, or at least there was no record of him having been under the influence of alcohol, although it is possible it played some minor factor in his actions; and so there had been no disagreement that had resulted in alcohol-fuelled violence. Why then did he commit two acts of murder?

As in many of these cases, it appeared Cross had acted as a consequence of deep-rooted mental illness, with one of its manifestations being paranoia. The killer had a history of mental illness stretching back at least two decades, when it was identified in 1826. Cross had been originally misdiagnosed as suffering from typhus, after having disappeared from his home in the night, wearing only a nightshirt. However, having failed to respond to treatment for the symptoms of that condition, it later emerged he was suffering from a psychological disorder. When this was recognized in 1826, he was placed in the Spring Vale Lunatic Asylum, but released months later, following the birth of Matilda, in the belief that his condition had been successfully treated. It was thirteen years later, in 1838, that Cross again showed signs of mental health problems, and lost his job as a consequence. However, his problems had dropped beneath the surface by 1840, when he was working once again. The couple moved house to where the deadly attacks were committed and all was seemingly tolerable for the next six years.

It had only been in January 1847 that Cross' illness resurfaced and, as such, it is quite likely that none of those who lived near the Cross household would have been aware of his state of mental health. That month he paid visits to a long-time friend, with the visits becoming increasingly frequent. It was apparent that Cross had pressures on his mind and, eventually, towards the end of January, the concerns were discussed. He strongly believed, in fact had no doubt, that his wife was planning on killing him. He was convinced that Ann intended to poison him and he wanted to prevent this from happening. Ending his wife's life was the means by which he sought to preserve his own.

Osbourne was killed simply because she happened to get in the way. Presumably, with no thought of malice towards his own daughter, he had no intention of killing her or, perhaps more likely, she was simply lucky not to have been stabbed herself. It had been suggested that Cross's paranoia led to the belief his whole family were trying to kill him but it would appear his main fears centred upon his false perception of his wife's thoughts and intentions.

Charged with wilful murder, Cross was remanded. He appeared at the Derby Assizes in March 1847. There was no doubt he had caused the deaths, but a defence was put forward for him that he was not guilty of murder on the grounds of insanity. Naturally, the prosecution's case was that the prisoner had known exactly what he was doing when he planned to kill his wife, and that he had contemplated the crime for some time. Therefore, premeditation and malice were present in Cross' mind when he began his savage attack on his sleeping wife. His reasoning behind the attack may have been misplaced, but it was, quite simply, a case of murder, it was argued. It could further be argued that by having tried to prevent Louisa from entering the bedroom, he was fully aware of what he had done and was aware of the consequences of his actions. He was certainly not indifferent to what had taken place.

The surgeon of Derby Gaol, who had examined Cross during his time on remand awaiting trial, testified on behalf of the defence. He told the court that it was his belief that the defendant had suffered insanity at the time of his crimes. According to Douglas Fox, the prisoner did not know where he was when interviewed in the gaol. He had believed he was in the lunatic asylum he had been confined to two decades earlier. He denied any knowledge of having attacked Osborne who, at the time of the interview, was still alive but critically ill. The prisoner had a 'very insane appearance of the countenance', the surgeon added.

On the basis of this evidence, and knowledge of the defendant's medical history, the trial judge, Mr Justice Patterson, instructed the jury to find Thomas Cross not guilty on the grounds of insanity. Obligingly they did so and Cross was sent back to a lunatic asylum for the remainder of his days.

CHAPTER 14

Death in the Asylum
1849

A man named Harold Strelley, thirty years of age, who came from a respectable family, slept in the same room as a man named Samuel Tomlinson, in a private lunatic asylum kept by Dr Brigstocke, in Green Lane, Derby. Strelley had been in the asylum for approximately three months before any incident of note took place. One night, with the door locked from the outside so that neither man was able to leave, which was the usual practice for that room at the asylum, tragedy took place.

The keeper of the asylum slept in an adjacent room with other patients. At some time between 5 and 6am he heard noises coming from Strelley and Tomlinson's room and went to investigate. With a light he could see Tomlinson lying on the floor in a pool of blood, with Strelley standing in a corner of the room, blood on his hands and clothing.

Of course it was clear from the outset what had happened in terms of who was responsible. It transpired that Tomlinson had been getting dressed and whilst doing so he did or said something that caused fear in the mind of Strelley who, at that point in time, jumped out of his bed and stabbed his roommate with a lath from the bed; and which was later found covered in blood.

At trial at the Derby Assizes, on 16 March 1849, Strelley was found not guilty of murder on the grounds of insanity. He was sentenced to a lifetime within an institution similar to that in which he had killed. The judge condemned the owner of the asylum for allowing two insane men to share a room without supervision.

CHAPTER 15

The Singular Case of the Canal Child 1851

It was shortly before 8am, on Wednesday 3 December 1851, that William Calladine and Thomas Clarke, who worked at Smith, Cox and Co's cheese warehouse, became entangled in one of Derbyshire's most baffling unsolved murders. It was on opening the back door of the warehouse, which backed onto the bank of the canal, that Calladine saw what appeared to be a baby in the water, a little below Siddal's bridge. The men ran across the bridge and to the other side of the canal. 'Oh Lord, William, come here, it is a child!' shouted Clarke to his colleague, who was shortly behind him.

Older readers may recall traces of the canal in Derby city centre, and indeed some slight remnants of the infrastructure do survive in places, but much of the canal was filled and developed upon as Derby's appearance has changed over the past century, with progress altering the city to such an extent that even our most recent ancestors would not be able to recognize large areas. The water in the canal was, at the point where Calladine and Clarke had been drawn, only approximately one foot in depth. The area was popular with walkers and a large number of boats regularly passed along this stretch of the canal. Bringing the body out of the water, the men noticed that something was tied around the child's waist, and this was found to be a brick tied in a handkerchief, to weigh the body down in the hope that it would not be found.

The body appeared to be that of a girl who the men thought was probably aged about three years old but they did not inspect the body closely. Instead they took it to Mr Pearson's Railway Tavern on Siddall's Lane.

When found and whilst at the Railway Tavern, the girl was wearing clothes including shoes and socks. When examined, a piece of black lining was found to be tied around the child's neck, which would have contributed to causing her death, and post-mortem examination carried out by Henry Francis Gisborne revealed that the child had died of drowning. It was again thought the girl was about three years old. It was believed that the child had only been in the water for a few hours prior to her discovery.

It soon emerged that a woman had been seen with a child in her arms by a man, named Joshua Simpson, close to the spot where the body was later found, at between 6 and 7pm on 2 December. However, Simpson believed he would not be able to identify the woman he saw. It seemed certain to the police that the unfortunate girl was the same as that seen by Simpson and that the woman was the killer.

An inquest was held at which the evidence was presented that the child had been deliberately drowned. However, the child's identity was unknown and the inquest jury returned a verdict that the unidentified deceased girl was murdered by a person or persons unknown.

The child's identity and the identity of her killer were a complete mystery and so police investigations continued. Eventually the investigation centred on the Ilkeston area in light of new leads. The new information related to individuals who claimed they knew who the deceased girl was and those inquiries culminated in a twenty-five-year-old woman being questioned.

Following claims that the child found in the canal was named Maria Louisa Sudbury, it was decided to question her mother, Selina Ryde. This questioning took place in March 1852 by Constable George Small, at Ryde's home in Weston-Under-Wood, where she lived with her husband.

Selina Ryde had married Benjamin Ryde in August 1851. However, she had not at that time told her husband that she had a daughter. Indeed, it was not until two months after the marriage that Ryde's husband learnt he had a step-daughter. Maria had been an illegitimate child and, perhaps with some sympathy, one can understand that Benjamin Ryde did not want the child in his house. However, he agreed that he would pay for the child to be looked after. Following this arrangement having been made, Selina decided to try and get the child out of the Basford Union Workhouse where it had been living for some time. Her first application for the removal of the child was rejected because Maria was too ill. However, on 15 November 1851, Maria was allowed to be taken from the workhouse.

Upon removing the child, she was taken to Ryde's sister, Ann Wright. For the next seventeen days, Wright agreed to look after her niece for the sum of 1s and 6d per week for maintenance; a sum which was not paid in full. After seventeen days had elapsed, on Tuesday 2 December, at 11am, Wright took the child back to Ryde's house without warning, much to the latter's annoyance, because she could not afford to look after her on account of not having been paid the agreed sum. The mother did not know what to do with her daughter because she could not afford to have difficulties with her husband. At the time the child was taken back she was wearing a bonnet, a blue shawl, a white pinafore, a blue frock, a pair of slippers and socks.

During questioning, Ryde was asked where the child was, and Small was told that it was dead and buried in the cemetery at Derby. Ryde claimed that her husband was aware of the death and had even made the coffin.

Upon being told this, Small visited the cemetery and it was established that there was no record of a burial in any of the surnames of Ryde, Sudbury or the surname of the child's father, which was Sowrie. When questioned further, Ryde claimed a Mrs Smith had buried the child. When this was also shown to be untrue she changed the name again, claiming a nurse named Riley had buried the girl and that Riley had obtained a coffin, which contradicted the claim that her husband had made it. The inconsistencies in Ryde's story fuelled Small's suspicions, especially when all attempts to find a nurse named Riley were unsuccessful. On 17 March, Ryde was arrested on suspicion of the murder.

On 20 March, the body of the girl found in the canal was exhumed and examined once again. This was in order to confirm the identity of the girl as being Maria Sudbury. It had been suggested that the girl was Maria on the basis of the alleged presence of old scars on the deceased's breast and thigh; marks

St Peter's Church in Derby, where the canal child was buried in 1851 and exhumed the following year in a bid to establish its identity. The author

which were known to have been present on Maria's skin. A number of individuals who had known Maria believed they had seen such marks on the girl from the canal before she was buried. This second examination of the remains was undertaken upon exhumation at St Peter's churchyard and, despite some decomposition, it was concluded that the scars were not present. However, those who knew Maria also believed that the dead girl's hair and eyelashes were exactly the same as Maria's distinct eyelashes and hair. A number of people remained absolutely convinced that the girl was Maria Sudbury and therefore by inference Selina Ryde was a killer.

James Spencer, of Ilkeston, saw Maria every day whilst she lived with her mother in Ilkeston, before Ryde met her husband. He had examined the body after it was found in the canal. He told the magistrates, 'I could not recognise it by its features, but on examining it more particularly I saw scars, on its right side and I also saw another scar on the bosom which enables me to swear it was the child.'

Spencer's daughter, Ruth, agreed with her father, saying, 'I could not tell it by its features but by the scars on the body.

I knew it by these marks to be the child of Selina Sudbury and the one I had slept with and played with for rather more than a year.'

Ann Wright told the magistrates that the slippers found on the dead girl were 'similar to the ones worn by the child on the day I took her home to her mother. They are the ones she had on.' This suggested uncertainty because the word 'similar' is not the same as saying that they were indeed those shoes. However, in her argument she pointed to holes in the heels of the shoes and said there were holes in the shoes worn by her niece.

Ryde only spoke, out of all her court proceedings, to tell the magistrates that she did not kill her daughter: 'I am quite innocent – that is all I have to say,' she said, before being remanded into custody to await her trial. Whilst on remand she was weak and depressed. Reports claimed she was 'alarmingly ill' and there were even rumours that she had died.

The rumours were untrue, however, and the trial was held on 20 July 1852, at the Derby Assizes.

The prosecution, which was led by Mr Boden, said that if it could be proved that the child was the defendant's daughter and that she had been responsible for the death, then no matter how painful it was, the jury's duty to themselves and their country was to find her guilty. As such it had to be proven that both the deceased was Maria and that she had died at the hands of her mother.

Mary Anne Noon had seen the body on 3 December 1851 at the Railway Tavern and had believed it was Maria Sudbury. Noon had known Ryde for seven or eight years and knew the child also. At that point in time she had not informed the authorities of her belief, however, because another woman was at that time in custody on suspicion of it being her child, and so Noon believed she may have been mistaken in her identification. And so her belief did not come to the attention of the police until some months later.

The woman concerned, who had been in custody, had admitted to having a child but she told the officers that it was living with family in Leicester. Following the investigation of this claim, they were satisfied, with it being confirmed her child was indeed alive and well in Leicester, and so the woman was released. A second woman was arrested and several individuals claimed that she was the mother of the dead girl, but evidence was provided that her child was living with its father in Nottingham. Eventually, the child was brought, by her father, from Nottingham and that woman was also released without charge.

By the time of the trial some doubts had entered Ann Wright's mind. Wright said that shoes taken from the dead girl were not those which she knew Maria had worn. Maria's shoes were thought to be newer, although she again said that she recalled a hole in one of the shoes which was also present in the shoe from the body. Other items of clothing differed to those she had seen the girl wearing during the seventeen days she had looked after her, she said.

Wright also told the court that three weeks after she had returned the child to its mother, she had seen her sister in Derby market place and the child was not with her.

The defence argued that Ann Wright's evidence was open to question because she could not even correctly tell the court which month it was at the time of the trial, and she did not know whether it was July or another month or whether it was the beginning or the end of the month. How, therefore, could she be precise about the day she returned the child to its mother? How could she be precise about details such as holes in the shoes? Wright was able to argue, however, that she knew the date she had returned her niece because a neighbour by the name of Eliza Harrison had informed her of this date and the information was corroborated by other sources.

Kesziah Hunt testified that she had met Ryde on Christmas Day at Long Eaton Station. The child was not with her mother and Hunt was told that Maria was unwell and had been attended to by a surgeon.

Gisborne told the court he had not seen any scars such as those which had been said to exist on Maria's skin, whilst examining the flesh of the dead girl. However, he acknowledged that if the inch-long scar on the breast had been narrow, he may have failed to notice it. The larger mark on the thigh might not have been a permanent scar, he thought, and therefore may not have been visible because it had only been seen a long time before death. The absence of this mark on the dead girl was therefore not proof that the deceased was not Maria.

The defence argued that the accused woman had no motive to commit murder. She could, they argued, have placed her back in the workhouse. However, surely the fact that Ryde was unable to look after her child with her husband not allowing her to live in the house, and was annoyed that Maria was brought back to the house without giving her time to find alternative arrangements, was actually a motive. Ryde had not wanted her daughter in the workhouse, which is precisely why she had her removed in the November. It may have been no small task to have her re-admitted to a workhouse and, with little time, she may have panicked and resorted to murder.

It was argued that the clothes worn by the deceased girl had never been worn by Maria and, indeed, it was argued that the clothes and the body were far too small to be Maria. The jury was reminded that if they could not be satisfied that the drowned girl was Maria Sudbury, and they were told there was no proof she was, then they could not reach a guilty verdict.

The jury were not satisfied by the prosecution's evidence and after only five minutes of deliberation they returned a verdict of 'not guilty', much to the joy of many people within the court who gave applause. Ryde was carried from the dock in a state of insensibility.

The trial was over and Selina Ryde was a free woman, able to get on with her life but questions remain. Who was the girl found in the canal? Was it Maria? Was too much emphasis placed on the evidence of the scars to try and persuade the jury that it was not the defendant's daughter, even though the absence of scars was not absolute proof according to the medical evidence? If it was not Maria, then what happened to her and where was she buried? And irrespective of who the girl was, why was she killed? Due to a large amount of conflicting evidence these are questions that can never be answered.

CHAPTER 16

The Mysterious Case of Edward Marsh 1854

Edward Marsh's mother and sister were naturally concerned when they were told Marsh had been admitted to Derby Infirmary following an accident at work, yet the circumstances of how he became injured would be as mysterious as the identity of the man who took Marsh's life.

Marsh was a hard-working twenty-seven-year-old who lived with his mother and sister at the foot of Birley Hill, Birley (near Little Eaton), between Derby and Duffield. His job involved the repair of a bridge and he normally arrived home from work at 8pm. However, on Friday 25 August 1854, he failed to arrive. The following day the family were told of an 'accident'.

At around 4am on that Saturday, an engine driver had seen what appeared to be a body on the track. He was unable to investigate because the train could not be brought to a stop, but at the earliest opportunity he informed William Mansfield, the signalman, of what he had seen. Marsh was soon found and was still alive, but unconscious and heavily bleeding from a major head wound. He was taken to Derby on the morning mail train and admitted to the Infirmary, where he regained consciousness.

Between 5 and 6am Marsh was examined by two surgeons, Mr Douglas Fox and Mr Gisborne, both of whom noted two very serious scalp wounds. The skull had been fractured so badly that the brain was exposed in places, into which large fragments were embedded. Indeed, a piece of skull approximately half the size of an adult male's hand, was removed along with other fragments. There were no injuries to any other part of the man's body.

The railway track in Duffield close to where a pickaxe was stolen and further along which Edward Marsh was found seriously wounded in 1854. The author

Marsh remained conscious during this examination but was unable to speak at that time. However, it appeared he recognised his brother Henry. He was able to eat but the surgeons had little hope for his survival. It had been against the odds he had survived at all, let alone been conscious. He died on the Sunday night.

It was at first speculated that Marsh had been hit by a train; a reasonable line of enquiry given that he was found on a railway track. However, it was believed that had he been hit he would have suffered injuries on other parts of his body. Before he died Marsh was asked by Mary Lowe, a nurse at the infirmary, if he had been hit by a train. 'No, no', was his mumbled reply. He was unable to give any details as to how he came to be in his condition. It was suggested he might not have understood the question, but the totality of the evidence suggests he was not a train casualty. The police concluded that he must have been murdered, with his killer or killers having inflicted a blow to the head with tremendous strength before laying his body on the track to create the false impression of an accident.

There was sufficient evidence to support this conclusion. A pickaxe with blood on it was found near the scene. However, there was not much blood for such a serious wound, with only a small amount of blood on the shaft and no hair or skin, which one would have expected if it had been used to cause such a serious head injury. The shaft of the pickaxe had a dent on it, as if it had been struck against rails at the side of the track. Marsh's cap was also found twenty-one yards from his body, with a hole in it which corresponded exactly with the pickaxe. However, there was no head wound corresponding with the shape and size of the hole, suggesting the hole in the cap was created when Marsh was not wearing the cap, but it certainly suggested the pickaxe was connected to Marsh at around the time of his death. Close by, a section of hedge was found to have been broken, as if someone had quickly made an escape to an adjoining field and herbs beside the hedge had been trodden down, which led detectives to believe someone had been there waiting for some time.

Mansfield, the signalman, told the detectives that approximately a week before Marsh's death he had seen a man at some time between midnight and 1am, loitering around the track close to where Marsh's body was found. When he asked the man what he was doing, Mansfield was apparently given a 'saucy' answer. The stout man, who was wearing a brown coat, said he would come back and punch Mansfield's head off. Did this man kill Edward Marsh? Perhaps this encounter was merely a coincidence, but the man's identity was never established.

There were, however, doubts about the police's hypothesis. Gisborne told the inquest into the death that his initial belief had been that Marsh fell off a train, although what he was doing on a train in the first instance was not explained, unless he was trying to travel home by train, although there was never any evidence to suggest such an attempt was made. Gisborne later believed that the evidence was inconclusive; he could have been attacked or hit by a train but if he was attacked, given the nature of the fracture, he believed more than one blow would have been necessary. There was no evidence of more than one blow.

It has been said that Marsh usually arrived home from work at 8pm, but the attack did not take place until hours later.

Detectives were able to account for his movements leading up to his death, which were out of character but that is not to say they were necessarily of direct relevance to the reason as to why he died. He was seen at the Railway Tavern in Duffield, which stood opposite the stationmaster's house, close to the station, where he arrived at 7.30pm and drank seven pints of ale with a man named John Gamble, with whom he worked. The men left at 9pm and Marsh took a detour to accompany Gamble home. The men were later at the Woodhouse Tavern and were seen, by Elizabeth Woodhouse, to both be drunk. Marsh was apparently much worse than his companion. There was no quarrel between the two men, or involving the men and any other person, whilst they were present.

Gamble was investigated and eliminated and the police investigation failed to identify any credible suspect. It would appear that the killer followed his victim from the Duffield area. It was established that the pickaxe with the blood, which the police believed was the murder weapon, or at least was somehow used in the incident, had been taken from under what was referred to in the press as Duffield Road Bridge, in the village. William Foster recognised it as being one which he used in his work as a plate layer on the line near Duffield church, suggesting it was taken from the areas close to the railway station. He was able to confirm he had put the pickaxe under the bridge at 5.30pm on the Friday and that there had been no blood on it at that time. This suggests it was somehow involved in Marsh's death, even if it was not the main murder weapon. The fact it was taken from under the bridge and was found so close by to where Marsh was found makes this a certainty. It is inconceivable that a pickaxe could be stolen and later be found at a potential crime scene, with some blood upon it, and for that pickaxe to be entirely unconnected to the incident.

The police did not believe that Foster or any one of his colleagues were involved in the incident because there were four other pickaxes under the bridge which were better than the one which had been taken. It was their belief that anyone who used the tools would have taken one of the other four. This is a weak argument, however, and one hopes that the police looked further into the movements of each of the men before eliminating them.

The jury at the inquest before the coroner, Mr Balguy, deliberated for a few hours and reached a verdict that Edward Marsh was wilfully murdered by some person or persons unknown. This did not stop the speculation, however. A correspondent to *The Times*, calling themselves 'E P of Manchester' suggested that Marsh had caught his foot on the rail and fell. As for the hole in the cap, this could have been caused not by the pickaxe but by his head hitting the curved end of the guard which was perpendicular to the rails, E P believed. The cap could then have been blown to the side of the track.

Could E P have been correct? If so, how did the pickaxe come to be nearby and how did it come to have blood upon it? Could it be that Marsh stole the pickaxe for some unknown reason and was carrying out some illicit activity on the tracks? Was this death a result of misadventure rather than murder? It seems unlikely but the fact is we will never know. However, as far as the authorities were concerned this case remained one of Derbyshire's most baffling unsolved murders.

CHAPTER 17

The Murder of John Mayna 1855

In January 1855, John Mayna, a twenty-nine-year-old Irish labourer, was living in Sleet Moor, a secluded village near Alfreton. He was known to be an industrious man of thrift who had saved up a relatively considerable amount of money. He was generally respected but did not associate himself with his colleagues or the majority of those within his community. He had a reputation for saving and secreting large amounts of money and was regarded as being eccentric. Indeed, in January 1855, he had told Mr and Mrs Bradley, with whom he lodged, that he hid gold in his coat stitched up in the lining.

Later that same month, he set out to buy food for his supper, but he never made it to where he intended to go. As he walked he was waylaid by three men, at Sleet Moor Lane. There he was brutally beaten with rails from a nearby fence and left for dead.

William Rooth was returning from the colliery where he worked and as he passed Sleet Moor Lane he heard the breaking of wood and loud groans. Rooth went to a nearby cottage for help and returned to the scene with John Horsepool and two other men, bringing a light with them because although it was only 6pm it was a dark winter's evening.

A hedgestake was found covered in blood and in an adjacent field they found the injured man on the ground, immediately next to a 170-yard-deep coal-pit, located twenty yards from the road, with a trail of blood showing he had been dragged into the field. He was so close to the pit that it was said that if he had simply rolled over he could have fallen into it. One has to wonder why his attackers did not dump his body into it, to prevent any description being given of him and delay the commencement of any investigation. Perhaps they panicked or they believed he was dead or would never regain consciousness.

Mayna had been so badly beaten that his neighbour could not at first recognize him, although his identity was soon determined when he was taken to a beer house and recognised by some of the regulars.

Mayna was then carried to his lodgings but Mrs Bradley, who was alone with the children, did not dare open the door because she was unaware of who it was and so the unfortunate man was forced to lay outside for two hours until Mr Bradley returned. Upon being taken inside his home, Mayna's wounds were washed and treated but medical help was only sought the next day, which was too late, with Mayna then being informed by surgeon Mr Henderson that nothing could be done to save his life. He managed to survive a few days longer, but upon being told he was dying he agreed to make a statement in which he named three Irish men, Thomas Barrett, Thomas Wall and Michael Donnelly, as being those who had robbed and attacked him; but his details were vague. Before his death he named the men several times but gave no further details of what had happened, which might not necessarily have been surprising given his injuries and knowledge of his impending death, which would have caused tremendous shock.

Mayna's waistcoat and stitched money had been taken and so the motive was clear and it appeared that it was most likely that the crime had been committed by someone known to Mayna, who was aware of his wealth. It was a ferocious attack; his right temple, jaw, chin and head were all severely wounded with a heavy blunt instrument which was assumed to be the hedge-stake. His loins were also badly bruised.

On the basis of Mayna's statement, Superintendent James arrested the men. The inquest was concluded towards the end of January and the preliminary case against the three men was conveyed. The coroner, Mr Busby, expressed doubt about whether the declaration by the dying man against those he accused of killing him could be received as evidence but declared that the legalities would be determined in a higher court. The jury found a verdict of 'wilful murder' against Barratt, Wall and Donnelly, who were brought into the inquest room and protested their innocence.

There was no trial for the three men, however. They appeared at the Derby Assizes in March 1855 with an announcement made that they would stand trial at the next session in the summer. On 25 July, the three men again appeared at the assizes to have charges against them dropped as a result of a coroner's inquisition. It would seem that the authorities had a lack of evidence against them and that there were further reservations about the reliability of the dying victim's words, and the vagueness of his statement. Who murdered John Mayna and what happened to his money was a mystery which was never solved.

CHAPTER 18

Death in the 'Heat of Blood': The Killing of James Ratcliffe 1855

William Clarke, a twenty-two-year-old labourer, was drinking in The New Inn public house in Horsley Woodhouse, near Ilkeston, on the evening of Saturday 15 September. Also present was James Ratcliffe, of whom few facts were reported in the press, and a large number of other drinkers.

The nature of the atmosphere earlier in the evening is unknown, but certainly by 11pm tempers were frayed, no doubt as a result of the amount of alcohol consumed, and the night was to end with bloodshed, as alcohol-fuelled bravado filled the minds of both Clarke and Ratcliffe.

At some point in time between 11pm and midnight a scuffle began in the building. Clarke had begun to fight with another person present, who was not named at the trial or in the press reports of the incident. Ratcliffe intervened in the fight, trying to separate the two men. His efforts rebounded and, as is often the case, as a result he and Clarke began to fight. As the situation worsened a police constable was sent for and the public house was cleared. The hope that by dispersing the troublemakers and the innocent bystanders the problems would cease was to be thwarted.

Once the public house was cleared most of its patrons remained outside, loitering in the darkness of the night, whilst Clarke began to head for his home. With a grievance yet to be satisfied, Ratcliffe decided to follow him for a short distance before returning to the public house. Upon his return he told people that Clarke had pulled his nose during the struggle, causing some pain, and that if he clapped eyes on him again he would have a 'stroke with him' and see if he was really man enough to fight with him.

Clarke was later told by one of those who had heard the threat, that Ratcliffe 'was hunting for him'. With little or no evident concern, Clarke replied, 'If he comes I have something in my pocket to quiet him.' Upon being asked what he had in his possession that he would use, Clarke said he had a knife.

Events progressed at a quick rate, with it only being half an hour between The New Inn being cleared and Clarke and Ratcliffe meeting again outside. Presumably Clarke left his home after being told of Ratcliffe's drunken words and decided to confront him. There was a crowd in the darkened street and Clarke found that Ratcliffe was surrounded by people. When Ratcliffe saw Clarke his body language turned to one showing aggression, and Ratcliffe approached Clarke, striking him.

A bystander intervened, placing himself in between the two brawlers, but Ratcliffe pushed past and struck Clarke again, and a full fight broke out. Clarke was seen to put his left arm around Ratcliffe's neck and his right hand was seen going into his coat pocket, but apparently none of the witnesses knew what was about to happen due to the speed at which the situation developed. His hand was seen to leave his pocket and then strike Ratcliffe in his lower body. No one had seen the knife, perhaps not even Ratcliffe. By this point in time nobody had dared to intervene.

After a minute or two of the fight commencing Clarke fell to the ground and only then did the seriousness of the situation show itself to the spectators, when Ratcliffe moved away shouting 'He has stabbed me!' He had been stabbed in the abdomen so deeply that his bowels were seen to protrude from the wound. He was carried home and a surgeon arrived reasonably swiftly, noticing two further wounds on the thigh and abdomen. The medical assistance was inadequate due to the nature of the injuries sustained, although he survived in the short term, and Ratcliffe died three days later.

When arrested, Clarke denied having been in possession of a knife for a fortnight, but witnesses told the police that they had seen him with a pocket knife that day and the killer eventually admitted his ownership of the weapon. The above evidence was recounted for the benefit of the jury at Clarke's murder trial held on Thursday 6 December 1855. The defence told the jurors that there was no doubt Ratcliffe had died as a result of Clarke's actions. However, they argued that their client should be convicted of manslaughter rather than murder.

The judge, Mr Justice Creswell, in his summing up, asked the jury to consider whether this was a case of murder or manslaughter. He asked them to establish whether Clarke had acted with the desire to commit evil and whether he had a mind fatally bent on mischief, or whether his actions were given in the 'heat of blood', which 'was not to be referred to that malignant desire to do evils which was an essential ingredient in the crime of murder'. If the fatal blow was as a result of the attack made against him, and it was made in the 'heat of blood' then the law, making allowances for 'human infirmity', considered it not to be murder, the learned judge remarked. The judge reminded the members of the jury that certainly earlier outside The New Inn it was Ratcliffe who was making threats of violence regarding Clarke and being aggressive in his behaviour. One has to wonder whether other judges may have been so accommodating to a man who had returned with an altercation in mind, when he could quite simply have returned home and stayed there. During that half hour between the original altercation and the two meeting once again, Clarke had not been in any danger and if he had returned home the trouble may have been averted.

It took the jury fifteen minutes to reach their decision that Clarke did not have a desire to commit evil and that he was acting in response to the attack against him. He was found guilty not of murder but manslaughter and was sentenced to fifteen years' transportation. On 19 March 1857, Clarke, convict 4304, boarded the convict ship *Clara*, a 708-ton vessel used twice for transportation purposes, in London, along with 261 other convicts and ninety-five other passengers consisting of guards and their families. Other convicts on the same ship included one who received the same sentence as Clarke, but for stealing a mare, several men who received the same punishment for burglary or shopbreaking, a man who received twenty years of transportation for 'feloniously cutting and wounding with intent to prevent his lawful apprehension', and a man who received lifetime transportation for burglary, showing that the inconsistencies in sentencing is an age old problem contrary to what some may believe to be a modern issue with our justice system. The voyage lasted 106 days before *Clara* landed at Fremantle on 3 July. What became of Clarke once his fifteen years had been completed is unfortunately unknown.

CHAPTER 19

The Brutal Killing of Enoch Stone 1856

Enoch Stone was a forty-seven-year-old framework knitter, glove maker and a keen flute player, who occasionally led the choir at Spondon Church. Commonly known as 'Knocky', he was a man of few means and his work was only just sufficient to provide for himself and his family. His daughters also helped support the household, working at a local mill. When the daughters returned to the home they shared with Stone, at approximately 8pm on Monday 23 June 1856, they found him reading his Bible. Upon their arrival he immediately got up and left, saying he had to collect his son's dirty washing. There was nothing suspicious in his hasty departure upon their entrance; he was presumably waiting for them to return and wished to collect the washing and head home before it was too late.

Stone had been walking along Nottingham Road, along the stretch of road now named Derby Road, which at the time was not distinguished from the remainder of the Nottingham Road, when tragedy struck. He had been heading back to his home on Church Street in Spondon, carrying the laundry.

On his journey he had stopped off at the Plough Inn on Nottingham Road for a drink and some bread and cheese, leaving sober. He had then continued on his way, alone, and was last seen alive at 10.45pm by a tollgate keeper on the Nottingham Road, hobbling along. For twenty years he had suffered from crippling paralysis which caused him to walk very slowly. Two hours later a servant was heading towards Derby to collect his master, Mr W S Cox, when he caught sight of Enoch's basket with clothes scattered around. Heading in the opposite direction, a keeper with the surname Davis also noticed that something was amiss. Curious and concerned, the men investigated and soon discovered Enoch laying seriously injured on the ground at a point along Derby Road close to its junction with Oregon Way, in the Chaddesden part of the city. A small stone still stands, marking the spot where the man was found and where, presumably, he was mortally wounded. The stone was paid for by the community that was so shocked by the news of the disabled, defenceless man's brutal murder, and bears the initials 'E.S.', although the effects of the passage of time have made the letters less discernible. Enoch Stone Drive is another lasting tribute to the popular man.

The men may have had suspicions, but others certainly had not. A number of people who had passed by earlier had assumed that the groaning man was simply drunk and they had walked on by. A large festival, which had attracted between 20,000 and 30,000 visitors, had been held at Derby arboretum on the night of the attack and it was believed that a large number of people must have passed along Nottingham Road as a result. It was therefore hoped that there would be many useful witnesses who could provide evidence that would catch the killers.

The police made significant errors, however. Although the servant and Davis went to Derby to alert the police of the crime, officers failed to issue a notice and enquiries did not begin until later in the morning. The first few hours of a murder investigation are often crucial to its prospects of success. It is likely many of those who attended the festival would have left the area by the time enquiries commenced and would never have learnt that the crime had been committed. As such, a large amount of relevant information may never have come to the attention of the authorities.

It was clear that the disabled man had been viciously beaten about the head with a heavy, blunt instrument. Several pieces of bloodstained bark were found, and it was believed that a branch or block of timber had been used to cause the fatal injuries. His skull had been fractured and large volumes of blood were pouring from his extensive head wounds when he was found. Numerous pools of blood suggested he had been beaten and then dragged a few yards. It was believed that at least two individuals must have been involved in the vicious attack. The dying man's right hand pocket had been turned out,

The junction of Derby Road and Oregon Way, where Enoch Stone was attacked and mortally wounded. The author

A small stone erected at the point where Enoch Stone was violently attacked and left for dead. The author

Enoch Stone Drive, named in memory of the victim of one of Derby's most shocking unsolved murders of the Victorian period. The author

but it was estimated he had had only had 10d on his person when attacked. His boots, which were odd, had been stolen, and it was presumed a number of items of linen were also taken.

The dying man was taken to his home but the best efforts of a surgeon, Dr James Cade, failed to avert the onset of death. He died at 6am having never regained consciousness.

Several suspects were arrested in the early days of the investigation, but there was insufficient evidence against any of them. A woman had been seen on Nottingham Road, in the company of two suspiciously acting men. That woman was identified and when questioned on the Tuesday morning about her actions at the time of the attack, she gave a confused account in which she contradicted herself a number of times. Two Irish men were arrested when they were found in a field beside Nottingham Road, hours after the attack. It was believed they were the two men with whom the woman had been seen. One of the men had bloodstained trousers and the second man had bloodstains on his shirt. All three were released without charge.

A tramp named David Hall was arrested after he was seen carrying a pair of boots as he walked along Cemetery Hill. He was held for two weeks but was released when it was proven he had been in Bromsgrove on the day of the murder.

Even a well publicized £120 (about £5,000 in today's money) reward (£100 offered by the authorities and a further £20 offered by horrified members of the community who had been so affected by the crime) failed to encourage anyone with the crucial information to come forward. Accomplices who had not committed the murder itself were offered a pardon, but still no one came forward.

An inquest on 21 July at the Malt Shovel Inn, Spondon, recorded that Enoch Stone was murdered by person or persons unknown. The police investigation failed to alter that outcome.

CHAPTER 20

Killed for Three Eggs: The Death of Thomas Watts 1858

People have been killed for a variety of motives and often when the cause of the murderous intention has been so small that the taking of a life is harder to understand. A fight over three eggs cost a man his life and resulted in one of the most lenient sentences (for violently killing an unarmed man) in Victorian Derbyshire.

Shortly before midnight on Saturday 15 May 1858, Joseph Morley, a twenty-three-year-old collier, returned to his lodgings at Unstone, a small town approximately a mile from Dronfield, principally occupied by workers of the local pits, having been drinking at Bowers in the village. Upon arriving home he asked Mrs Kirkham for his supper, but much to his anger he discovered that the meal, which had consisted of three boiled eggs, had already been eaten by Thomas Watts. The latter, who

The small town of Unstone, near Dronfield, where Morley and Watts fought over three eggs in 1858. The author

also lodged in the same house, was sat on a chair near the fire whilst Morley asked for more eggs to be cooked for him. Upon making his request Morley then sat on the hearthstone.

According to Morley's statement, which he made to a police sergeant shortly after his arrest, the situation quickly became violent. Watts became enraged and tried to force Morley out of the lodgings. 'Watts got out of his chair and began to beat me. I called on the other lodgers to take him off me but they did not offer to take him away. I then took hold of my pocket knife. I don't know whether I took it out of my pocket or not, but I had it in my hand and I stabbed Watts. I cannot say how many times.'

It was three times that Morley had stabbed Watts during the course of the fight; once in the left armpit, once on the left breast and a final wound on the left thigh. The chest wound caused the fatal injuries having penetrated the ribs and cut part of the heart.

After fatally wounding his fellow lodger, and with the blood on his hands, the killer went to bed. Meanwhile the local parish constable, William Gill, arrived to arrest Morley.

Upon being arrested, as part of his statement, he said, 'I did not intend to take his life. I meant to wound him severely. I am very sorry I have done it.' Of course, Morley had to defend himself from Watts' attack but the victim was unarmed and Morley suffered no injury or serious threat to his life by Watts' actions.

In today's society, and indeed since the Homicide Act was passed in 1958, murder has been defined as an act of intentionally killing a person or carrying out an act of violence with the motive of causing serious harm, which results in a person's death. Even without the experience of the subsequent century to guide them, it is unsurprising given the circumstances that the jury at the inquest returned a verdict of wilful murder against Joseph Morley.

Morley was lucky, however. At his trial at the Derby Assizes in July 1858 the jury returned a verdict of 'guilty of manslaughter'. Watts' life, and the manner in which it was ended, was thought to be worth only two years and it was for this period of time that Morley was sentenced, with the first and last week of that incarceration to be in solitary confinement.

CHAPTER 21

Three Months for a Life: The Death of Edwards 1858

It was the night before Christmas in 1858, at the Bishop Blaize public house in the Morledge area of Derby, but festivities were brought to a tragic end and resulted in an even shorter sentence than that handed down to Joseph Morley. Two of the regulars at the public house, Arthur Bland and a man named Edwards (whose first name was not recorded), were drinking together inside. They had been drinking since about 11am. Bland had once been in the militia but he was not a respectable man. He was a poacher who had a criminal record for theft and ran a house of 'ill fame'. Edwards lived with Bland's sister but despite the feelings of the sister the two men did not get on well and regularly quarrelled. It was no surprise that on that night they would not honour the season of goodwill.

Indeed by the late afternoon matters had begun to get out of hand. They went into the yard at some time between 4 and 5pm and had three or four rounds of fighting, but this was brought to an end by the landlord, Mr Pool. They returned indoors, shook hands and continued drinking. The fight had been started when Bland was hit with a candle by a woman. In retaliation Bland had hit the woman in the mouth, resulting in Edwards demanding a fight. Apparently earlier that day Bland had threatened to kill Edwards. Edwards told his opponent he was a better man than Bland and the fight commenced.

During the struggle both men had got dirty. Whilst in the Bishop Blaize, following the fight, James Birch saw Bland stood between two tables, using a clasp knife to scrape dried mud off his trousers, and so he already had a knife in his hand.

Any relief which Pool had had was short-lived, however, when Edwards hit Bland on the head, knocking him over. Bland then lunged at Edwards with the knife, stabbing him just beneath the chin. There was a gush of blood and the injured man moaned 'Oh I am stabbed.' He was dead when the surgeon arrived approximately five minutes later.

William Tarr seized hold of Bland until the police arrived. He was apprehended by Sergeant Davis who searched him and found the bloodstained knife. The killer claimed to be innocent, telling the sergeant, 'I know nothing about it. It is not my knife.' He claimed someone had planted the knife in his pocket but could offer no suggestions as to who did so. Such a claim was quite bizarre and desperate given the number of witnesses who had seen him kill Edwards, and the blood which no doubt covered his clothing.

The post mortem, undertaken by Dr Gisborne, found that the wound had been an inch long and was immediately below the prominent part of the windpipe, which was completely severed, and that the wound protruded to a depth of three inches extending to the muscles in the back of Edwards' neck.

The jury at the inquest concluded that Edwards had died as a result of manslaughter committed by Bland, on the grounds that he was provoked. The trial jury reached the same verdict on 17 March 1859 and he was sentenced to just three months' imprisonment.

CHAPTER 22

Buried in a Shallow Grave
1862

An act as simple as allowing a dog to wander through a field resulted in an awful discovery one Thursday morning in early September 1862. The dog became alerted to a scent and began scratching at the ground in a field owned by Henry Locker, the farmer of a small piece of land at Derby. Very soon after the dog began to dig into the soil it started to uncover a bundle wrapped in a handkerchief. Upon examining it, the dog's owner, a man named Fletcher, noticed that the handkerchief contained another layer of wrapping, consisting of brown paper. Inside the parcel was the corpse of a newborn baby boy. The police were immediately contacted and were quickly on the scene.

The brown paper was carefully cleaned to reveal the words 'Locker, Derby' written on it. It was immediately clear that there was a connection to Locker's household and/or his staff. The head constable, Mr Hilton, believed the killer must have had some connection to the farm, with access to the paper bags. With Inspector Fearn, Hilton went to the farm to speak with Henry Locker.

Their visit met with interesting clues sooner than they had anticipated. The two detectives noticed that upon their arrival the domestic servant, a respectable looking girl called Martha Dovey (also known as Martha Dooley and her surname was occasionally misspelt as Davey), who was just leaving the property, turned pale and hurried back into the house where she started frantically rubbing a table in an attempt to appear that she was busy working. This suspicious behaviour was not challenged at first, however, with the two policemen asking the whereabouts of Henry Locker. Only when told, by Locker's wife, that he was not at home did the detectives begin questioning the servant. It quickly transpired she was being evasive in her responses to the questions and so a search was commenced of her room.

Upon heading to Dovey's bedroom, Henry Locker was seen but the detectives were now convinced they would reach a satisfactory conclusion to their investigation by pursuing the servant girl. Entering the bedroom, bloodstained linen was observed and Martha Dovey was arrested and taken into custody on suspicion of murder.

Within a short period of time she confessed that she was the mother of the child and had given birth to it on 14 August. Upon its birth she had put the baby in the paper bag and had placed it in a shed for two days before burying it in the shallow grave. She claimed she had been unaware of whether or not the child was alive, had never heard it cry and seemingly had no interest in her offspring, not even knowing what sex it was.

Dovey was charged with the wilful murder of her illegitimate child on Saturday 30 August 1862. However, at her trial at the March Assizes in 1863 luck presented itself to Dovey more than it had to many of her contemporaries. She was convicted not of murder but only of the lesser offence of concealment of birth. She was sentenced to just one day's imprisonment.

CHAPTER 23

Suspicious Deaths and Unidentified Victims of the Nineteenth Century 1860-1879

In November 1866, the body of a man was discovered, floating in the River Derwent close to Little Eaton, near Derby, in the vicinity of the paper mills owned by Messrs Tempest.

Upon undertaking a post-mortem examination of the body it was determined that he had sustained violent blows to the back of his head, which had caused his death. The body had been in the water for several days. His pockets had not been emptied, and they contained letters which suggested the man's name was Francis Martin and that he came from Mapperley in Derbyshire. He was, it was discovered, a miller in a respectable position.

Due to the lack of evidence the inquest, before the coroner, Mr Whiston, returned an open verdict that Martin had been 'found drowned'.

Although Martin's identity was known there were a large number of murders and probable murders in nineteenth-century Derbyshire where the identity of the deceased and their killer or killers was never established, some of which are outlined here. Many of these unfortunates were found in the canals or rivers of the county, whilst others were discovered after a vain attempt at concealment or with no effort at concealment at all. It seems remarkable in this country that there could be so many un-identified corpses but, without an identity due to an absence of mechanism by which information could be spread across the county, and with many not realizing that someone they knew was pregnant and so a new born child would not always be missed. It was a time when people could claim their offspring had gone to live with family in another part of the country and it would not always be questioned.

In addition to the absence of the identity of a murder victim, or suspected murder victim, there was often the problem that a body dumped in a river, canal or other isolated location meant that the crime scene was either unknown, if the murder took place at a location different to that where the body was discovered, or that the crime scene did not normally have any association with an individual.

The difficulties were compounded further if the body had been discovered at a significant time after death, rendering it not only unlikely that an identity could be provided but also that a cause of death could not always be established.

One Friday evening at the beginning of March 1860, at approximately 8pm, a woman who lived in a court off Orchard Street in Derby was walking along a passage towards her home when, in the spring darkness, she 'trod on something soft'. Curious as to what she had stepped on, she went and got a light and carried the soft bundle to a neighbour's house where it was unwrapped. Upon removing the dark merino woollen cloth they were horrified to discover they had found a dead, newborn baby. The police were contacted and the body taken away.

Dr Johnson examined the corpse first and found it to be a baby that had been alive upon delivery, as opposed to it having been stillborn. Mr Hamilton, who undertook a post-mortem, confirmed this but no cause of death was recorded in the newspaper articles of the time.

The jury at the inquest before the coroner, Mr Vallack, returned a verdict of 'wilful murder against some person or persons unknown'. There was never any evidence uncovered as to how or by whom the body came to be in the passageway; the child's identity, like its killer, was never discovered.

On Tuesday 22 September 1863, the body of a respectably dressed girl, who appeared to have been only a few days old, was found in the River Wye near Buxton. The child was dressed in a long white frock, a long flannel body garment, with a linen band round the waist. It had a brown gauze veil tightly fastened around the neck and death was determined to have been caused by strangulation, presumably with the veil acting as a ligature. Enquiries were undertaken in Derbyshire and in towns from where trains had travelled to Buxton. The investigation could not determine the identity of the child or its killer, and an inquest found that it was a case of 'wilful murder by person or persons unknown'.

On Tuesday 21 January 1868, at 11am, a man was travelling down the Derby and Nottingham canal in a boat when he saw something floating in the water at the back of Mr Greensmith's flour mill on Nottingham Road.

Taking a closer look he was startled to discover he had found the body of a dead man. The man was wearing a shirt with his trousers taken down. The corpse was taken for examination and was found to have a cord and part of a muffler tied tightly round his neck. A large gash had been inflicted under his right ear and there was a second cut to his groin. There were several other cuts present on his arms and legs and one of his thighs had been dislocated.

It was thought the body had been in the water for several days. Despite an investigation the man's identity and that of his killer or killers was never established.

On Sunday 3 July 1870, Charles Torres of Union Street, Derby, and Patrick Anthony, a moulder of City Road, were walking along the side of the canal near Holland's Bridge at Chaddesden when they noticed a bundle in the water. As they approached they saw that the bundle was tied with rope and upon pulling it from the water it was soon established that the rope had not only been used to keep the bundle fastened, but also that a large stone weighing five and a half pounds had been tied to one end in order to weigh it down.

Taking the bundle to the side of the canal, the men opened it, unwrapping the three cloths (one of which was a table cloth), and were horrified to see the badly decomposed remains of a

SUPPOSED CHILD MURDER NEAR DERBY.

Yesterday (Monday) evening, Mr. Coroner Whiston held an inquest at Mr. Robotham's, George Inn, Midland road, Litchurch, Derby, on the body of a male child, found in the Nottingham canal, near Derby, on Sunday morning last. From the evidence adduced, it appeared that a man named Charles Torrs, who lives in Union street, Siddall road, Derby, in company with a man named Paul Anthony, a moulder, residing in City road, were walking on the side of the Nottingham canal, on Sunday morning last, when they perceived a bundle in the water. They drew it to the side, and on cutting the rope which bound the bundle found it contained the dead body of a male child. Attached to the bundle by a rope was a large stone, which, with the clothes of the child, were produced at the inquest. There was a white cloth wrapped round the child's mouth. Having taken the child out of the water it was conveyed to the police-station, at Litchurch. From the evidence of Mr. Gentles, who made a *post mortem* examination, it was to be gathered that there were no external bruises. The body appeared to him to have been in the water several days, but decomposition had advanced too much to determine the cause of the child's death. The lungs were fully inflated and the internal organs perfectly healthy, but it was his opinion that death had taken place before the child was put in the water—An open verdict was returned of "Found dead.'

An article from the *Derby Mercury* on 6 July 1870 regarding the suspected murder of an unidentified child found in the Nottingham canal. Author's collection young boy with a white cloth wrapped very tightly around his mouth. The body was taken first to the Town Hall and then to Litchurch police station, and a murder investigation began.

The attempt to dispose of the body, with the stone to weight it down, had been ill conceived. With decomposition, gases had built up causing the body to rise to the surface of the water.

A post mortem, undertaken by Mr Gentles, established the full extent of the decomposition. In addition to skin peeling from the child's face and legs, the internal organs appeared to have been healthy, although the brain had entirely decomposed. There were no signs of external injuries and the cause of death could not be established due to the poor state of the remains. It was Gentles' opinion that death had taken place prior to the child having been dumped in the canal, and that it had been in the water for four or five days.

Despite the suspicious circumstances, not least the presence of a cloth wrapped around the boy's mouth, the jury at the inquest at the George Inn on Midland Road, Litchurch, held on the day after the discovery of the boy, returned an open

The River Derwent in Derby, the scene of many suspicious deaths and unsolved murders. The author

verdict and recorded that the child had merely been 'found drowned'. His identity and the identity of the individual or individuals involved in his death and deposition remain a mystery.

On Saturday 15 April 1879, Robert Stevens, a labourer working at the Midland New Carriage Works in Derby was at the side of the River Derwent when he saw what was quite clearly a baby in the water. He grabbed a rail and, with the assistance of a boy named Laurence Grundy, managed to eventually bring the body to the side of the river where he was able to bring it out of the water.

If they had any hopes of saving a life, their hopes were in vain. The child had been long dead and was badly decomposed. It had blood on its head and it was covered in mud and dirt. A handkerchief, with the name 'W Shardlow' upon it, was found tied loosely around the baby's neck. Stevens sent his brother to fetch the police and the body was taken for examination.

When examined by Mr Copestake, Mr Cade and Mr Westwood, it was established that the boy was newly born and had been in the water for a period of between three weeks and a month. It had suffered bleeding to the scalp and there was a large amount of blood on the brain. There was no evidence that death was due to drowning or strangulation, despite the handkerchief. It was concluded that death had been the consequence of a fracture to the skull caused by great force. It may, the doctors believed, have been possible that such an injury was the result of

SUPPOSED CHILD MURDER IN DERBY.

On Thursday W. H. Sale, Esq., Deputy-coroner re-opened an adjourned inquest at the White Swan Inn, Spondon, on the body of a child which was found floating in the canal near Spondon.—Robert Stevens, a labourer at the Midland New Carriage Works, at Derby, said that last Saturday he was in the osier bed in the occupation of his uncle, Samuel Stevens, situate by the side of the river Derwent, at Spondon, when he saw a baby in the water, caught amongst the bushes by the side of the river. He got a rail and drew the body to the side, and a boy named Grundy took it out of the water. The child was all over mud, and appeared to have some blood on its head, and had a white handkerchief tied round its neck in a loose way. The handkerchief, on being washed, was found to have upon it the name " W. Shardlow." It was done in one corner apparently from a stencil-plate. Witness sent his brother for the police, and left the body with Lawrence Grundy. The body was in a very decomposed or decayed condition.—Mr. W. G. Copestake, surgeon, of Derby, said that on the 15th inst., accompanied by Mr. T. C. Cade, and Mr. H. C. Westwood, surgeon, of Spondon, he made a *post-mortem* examination of the body, in accordance with instructions from the coroner. After washing off all the mud and dirt, he found the body to be that of a recently born male child of full period. From the appearance of the body he was of opinion that it had been immersed in the water for a period of from three weeks to a month. On removing the scalp he found it bruised all over, and under it a considerable quantity of extravasated blood. The right parietal bone had a fracture across it of 4 inches in length; and the left parietal bone, one of two inches in length. On removing the bones of the skull, he found a large quantity of blood on the surface of the brain, extending to the base of the brain. After describing other appearances which he observed, he said there was nothing to indicate that the child had died from either strangulation or drowning. He was of opinion that it died from fracture of the skull, caused during lifetime, and before immersion, and by great violence. The fracture might have been caused by a fall, but it was not at all probable.—Mr. H. C. Westwood, surgeon, having given evidence, the jury came to the conclusion that the child died from fracture of the skull, but that there was no evidence how or by what means the fracture was caused.

An article from the *Derby Mercury* on 23 April 1879 regarding the inquest into the death of an unidentified child found in the River Derwent. Author's collection a fall, although they felt this was unlikely. Even if a fall did take place it did not explain how the child came to be in the river and its death not reported and an effort made by some individual to present the false impression of death by strangulation (although the handkerchief may have had some role in the death even if it was not the murder weapon).

The inquest jury at the White Swan Inn in Spondon concluded that death was the consequence of a fracture but that there was no evidence of how it happened and so they could not conclude it was a case of murder despite the suspicious circumstances of the body's deposition. The boy and his potential killer were never identified.

CHAPTER 24

'A Lamentable Tragedy': The Murder of Elizabeth Caroline Goodwin 1863

The murder of Elizabeth Goodwin generated more publicity than most murders in Victorian Derbyshire. This was not due to the nature of the crime, for the murder itself was no more extraordinary than many which have taken place in Derbyshire over the course of history, but because of the social status of the victim, her family and the culprit, and the way in which the justice system treated him. Yet remarkably little has been written of this fascinating case since the Victorian period.

Miss Elizabeth Goodwin was the granddaughter of Captain Francis Green Goodwin of Wigwell Hall near Wirksworth and it was close to the hall where Elizabeth's life was prematurely brought to an end. A native of Chester, Elizabeth Goodwin had moved in with her grandfather when she was about twenty years of age. Captain Goodwin was one of Derbyshire's oldest magistrates at eighty-four years old and, of course, the family were considerably well off and well respected by their peers. They lived beyond simple comforts but pain was to enter their lives on Friday 22 August 1863 when the twenty-two-year-old was killed in a horrific way by a man whom she had told she would no longer marry.

On the Thursday night, George Victor Townley, a Manchester cotton spinner, left his home city by train and travelled to Derby where he stayed in the Midland Hotel. The following morning he took the train to Whatstandwell, a few miles from Wirksworth, and obtained a room for the night at the Bulls Head Inn (now the Derwent Hotel), near the station. There he

Wigwell Grange, formerly known as Wigwell Hall, the home of the Goodwin family and close to where Elizabeth Goodwin was mortally wounded in 1863. The author

The Derwent Hotel in Whatstandwell, known as the Bulls Head Inn when George Townley left his belongings there before heading to Wirksworth in 1863. The author

took from his carpet bag a morphine pill and drank a glass of brandy, in an attempt to calm his emotions.

Townley was about twenty-five years of age and from a well respected family from Hendham Vale near Manchester. He was of 'a most gentlemanly bearing', according to press reports, being 5ft 9 inches tall. He was described also as being a mild mannered man who had been a great scholar and linguist. Captain Goodwin's brother had been his family physician and it was through this association that he made the acquaintance of Miss Goodwin.

After attempting to calm his nerves, Townley walked to Wirksworth and had more brandy en route before visiting Reverend Herbert Harris, the master of Wirksworth Grammar School, at about 1.30pm.

Harris knew Townley and had first seen him six or seven months previously. Townley explained to the Reverend the reason for his latest visit to the town. Reverend Harris listened as Townley informed him he had been engaged to Goodwin for a while, having proposed to her shortly before she moved to Wigwell Hall, but that she had written to him breaking off the engagement and asking that her letters be returned. He added that he wanted to see her so that he could hear from her own lips that their plans to marry were over and until then he would not be able to accept the heartbreaking news. However, his request to see his ex-fiancé had been refused. The Reverend later recalled that his visitor appeared to be relatively calm and collected as he explained the situation.

Townley had been told, by Goodwin, that she had become romantically attached to a clergyman who, unlike him, had the blessing of her family. The couple had met during the summer of 1863 and were engaged within weeks. Goodwin had accepted the clergyman's offer of marriage because she would not have to wait as long to marry him as she would for Townley. The Reverend confirmed that a clergyman had been visiting but would not reveal the name and suggested he write to arrange an interview or go to Wigwell Hall and try to speak to Miss Goodwin.

'Sooner or later I must see her,' he said to the Reverend in way of explanation. 'I have set her free but I must hear from her own lips that she gives up the engagement. She is of age and of liberty to please herself. I know I am not a good match and I do not wish to stand in her way.'

Townley later returned to speak to Reverend Harris at about 4.30pm and was again advised to write to her to ask that he may see her or visit that evening. This advice he followed, requesting the chance to speak to her and was granted time, so he visited later that day.

When Townley arrived at Wigwell Hall at about 5.30pm Elizabeth Poyser, the housekeeper, admitted him, having been instructed to do so by Goodwin. Goodwin and Townley soon went to the gardens to talk and were seen by Poyser who had been asked to make tea and when it was ready she went to tell Goodwin that tea was served. When tea was served Poyser claimed that Goodwin had confided that Townley had told her during the visit that if she did not accept his proposal then he would make sure that she could not marry anyone else. Prior to coming for tea Goodwin read the newspaper to her grandfather. After tea she went to meet Townley again, having agreed to do so prior to her departure for tea, despite warnings from Poyser in the grounds.

The pair went for a walk and were seen on the turnpike road at approximately 7pm and it appeared Goodwin was bidding him farewell. An amicable parting was not an option for Townley.

It later emerged that as they had walked, Townley had asked Goodwin to go away with him. He had previously written to her, following the knowledge of the break up, writing that it was his intention to go abroad. In that letter he had also said: 'It never rains but pours. I have had a strange run of luck lately,' before adding that the breaking up of the engagement was the latest in a series of recent problems. When she refused to travel with him, Townley put his arm round her neck and thrust the knife into her throat. He turned the knife round with force, breaking part of the blade.

Soon afterwards, Reuhen Conway, a farm labourer, heard a low moan as he walked towards Wirksworth. Upon investigating the source of the noise he found Goodwin on the roadside in the lane near the hall. She was trying to walk towards the hall, using the wall to support her as she staggered with blood on her face. 'Take me home, there's a gentleman down there that cut my throat,' she begged. He put his arms round her and helped her walk twenty yards before putting her down, at which point Townley walked towards him. The labourer asked the 'gentleman' if he was the one who stabbed her. 'I have stabbed her. She has proved false to me,' came the matter of fact response. He went back to Goodwin with Townley. Realising that she was dying, Goodwin begged to be taken to the Hall.

Unable to carry her himself, Conway went for help and as he did, leaving her with Townley, he saw the attacker bend down and kiss his victim's cheek saying, 'Poor Bessie.' He also tried to tend to her wounds.

The labourer returned with help and was relieved to see that Goodwin was still alive. Others approached and asked who was responsible and to each enquirer Townley admitted his guilt. To James Conway, presumably a relative of the farm labourer, he said, 'I have done it and I shall be hung for it.' Goodwin was told to pray for mercy for her soul as she was certain she was dying. Townley insisted on helping to carry her and her body was taken into the kitchen, where she died.

When Captain Goodwin was told of his granddaughter's death he asked the killer why he had done it. 'She has deceived me, and the woman who deceives me must die. I told her I should kill her. She knows my temper,' he replied to the shocked magistrate who had most probably never heard such a thing in all his years on the bench. The two men went into the drawing room and, with considerable restraint on the part of the elderly Captain, they had tea and also drank some water and brandy.

Dr Newton Mant was sent for, as was Police Constable Parnham, who took Townley into custody. Townley appeared cool and calm and did not show any signs of madness or rage. Mant, a Wirksworth surgeon, believed that by the time he arrived Goodwin had been dead approximately twenty minutes. There were three wounds caused by something such as a large clasp pocket knife with a six-inch blade, such as that found in the possession of Townley. The wounds were located on the right side of her neck, about three inches in length extending down towards the spine and dividing the principal vessels of the throat, one behind the ear, and a third which penetrated the left shoulder joint. Death was caused by excessive bleeding.

Parnham said he was sent for at 9.45pm on Friday evening and saw Townley, who said he wished to give himself up for murdering Goodwin. Townley added, 'Please do remember that I gave myself up.' Upon being asked if he understood the charge he confirmed that he did, and requested that he be allowed to see Goodwin, which he was permitted to do. He stood by her for a minute and a half without speaking.

He was then taken to the lock-up, on the way to which he said, 'I feel far more happier now than I did before I did it and I hope she is so.' After making this somewhat tasteless comment he changed the topic of conversation to the weather and other small talk, appearing to be quite calm in his demeanour. He was searched at the lock-up and amongst other possessions including letters, a liquor flask and watch, he handed over the bloodstained knife.

With his own admission and with compelling evidence the inquest jury inevitably reached the verdict of 'wilful murder against George Victor Townley' and he was committed to the next assizes at Derby.

On the Monday, following a weekend in the lock-up, he was brought before the Moot Hall at Wirksworth to be formally

The Old Lock-up in Wirksworth, where George Townley was taken after murdering Elizabeth Goodwin in 1863. The author

committed for trial by the magistrates. He was then taken by cart to Derby Gaol where he spoke with his distressed father. Although Townley accepted that he had killed the woman he had hoped to marry, he always maintained he had no intention of committing the crime until he did so, contrary to the evidence of the housekeeper.

As Townley awaited his trial, Goodwin's funeral took place towards the end of August. It was well attended, and the local shops paid their respects by closing and lowering their blinds. Elizabeth Goodwin was laid to rest at the cemetery at North End, Wirksworth.

Prior to the trial commencing, in October 1863, some further drama took place when it emerged that Wigwell Hall had been burgled and the culprit was none other than a discharged police superintendent, who had several of the stolen items in his possession when caught.

The trial opened on Friday 11 December 1863, with a packed courtroom. Counsel was composed of Mr Boden QC for the prosecution, Mr Macauley QC for the defence along with Mr Serjeant O'Brien and Mr Stephens. The identity of Goodwin's killer was not in contention, the court was told. It was merely the issue of the accused man's frame of mind that was to be decided upon.

Evidence was presented by Dr Forbes Winslow and others to determine whether the defendant had suffered from insanity at the time of the incident, which would establish whether he was guilty of murder or manslaughter.

Mary Townley spoke of the eldest of her three sons as being a gentle and humane man. She believed the letter he had received on 11 August had turned his mind, otherwise he would never have acted with any violence, let alone murderous actions. According to the mother, the letter (which Captain Goodwin burnt before the trial) referred to Miss Goodwin having met a clergyman whom Goodwin described as the most delightful man she had ever met and whom the Captain believed she should marry. Captain Goodwin had learnt that they were still corresponding and was wild with fury about it. The letter had stated, 'I want you to release me that I may have it to say that I am free. Do not take this too badly' and had closed with 'yours affectionately', which appeared to be a cold closing, in

Townley's opinion. The following day he did not eat and was given one eighth of a grain of morphine to control his nerves.

The judge, Mr Baron Martin, summed up the evidence for almost two hours, commenting that he could not recall a case where the facts had been clearer. That Townley had killed Goodwin was in no dispute, he said. The only issue for the jury to consider was the defendant's state of mind. Did he wilfully commit murder or was he guilty of manslaughter? There could be no doubt that he had been affected by news that the engagement was off, the judge said. He had been seen muttering to himself and appeared greatly distressed. However, a witness in Wigan who he had spoken to, after receiving the letter, noted nothing particularly unusual about him. And Mr Harris who conversed with him at length, whilst noting he was upset did not see any signs of mental illness. He seemed to be aware of his actions and following the crime he had repeatedly said that by taking a life he had broken the law, had broken the commandment 'thou shalt not kill' and that he would be hanged as a result. He could therefore distinguish between right and wrong and was fully aware of the consequences for what he had done. From the outset he knew, and remarked upon the fact, that he would be arrested and sent for trial. When asked about letters in his possession, written by the deceased, he had told the Captain, 'You may read them, burn them, do what you like with them. I don't want them to be brought into court.' Therefore he had a good grasp on reality, immediately after his crime, and was aware of the seriousness of what he had done at that time. This was entirely inconsistent with the suggestion that he had experienced insanity, the judge remarked.

The jury accepted that Townley had borne no signs of insanity and after only five minutes of consultation they returned a guilty verdict. Upon being asked if he had anything to say following conviction Townley only lowered his head and remained silent.

Mr Baron Martin then donned the black cap and told the convicted murderer:

George Victor Townley, after everything that could possibly be urged in defence of your crime has been done in an ability never excelled the jury have found you guilty of murder and I am bound to say that in that verdict I entirely concur, for if the defence that has been set up in your behalf was allowed to have prevailed it seems to me it might have been attended with the most disastrous consequences to the country and if it did become instilled into the minds of young men that they were justified in taking away the life of a young woman who transferred her affections to another, the consequences indeed would be dreadful.

The learned judge stumbled over the words, 'May the Lord have mercy on your soul.' Townley left the dock seemingly unmoved.

For whatever reason, and it was speculated by many that his position of relative privilege helped, Townley was never executed for his crime. Despite what he said in his summing up and sentencing, Mr Baron Martin recommended that an inquiry be carried out to assess the killer's state of mind, based on Martin's view that Townley's demeanour at trial had been unusual.

On 26 December, the Commissioners for Lunacy visited Derby and had two lengthy interviews with Townley. They also interviewed the Governor (who was convinced the killer was sane), the warders, the prison surgeon and Townley's parents. They noted that he seemed more at ease since his conviction and was occasionally cheerful. They considered his justification of the murder on moral grounds to be 'extraordinarily perverted' and noted there was insanity in the family, with his grand-mother having exhibited signs of an unsound mind. However, the commissioners concluded that 'his views of right and wrong, false as they are, appear to have been coherently acted upon and with a full sense of what they involved.'

Townley had said during the interviews, 'What have I been guilty of? I don't admit I am guilty of anything. I don't believe that I have done any harm. Bessie Goodwin was my property, and I had a right to do what I did because she was false to me. I was not myself when I did it. I might have been mad at that moment. I am quite sane now. I have done her no harm. She is better where she is than if she had lived.' He added that he considered his relationship with Goodwin to be on a par with marriage and that a man has a right to kill his wife if she is adulterous.

The Commissioners found that Townley was correctly convicted. The Visiting Judges, however, ruled that the manner in which the Commissioners had operated was wrong because their inquiry had been conducted in private. They requested that a full public inquiry should be undertaken. This was supported by a large number of people, including many members of the clergy. Eventually it was ruled that Townley was insane and his death sentence was commuted to one of life imprisonment. He was taken to Bethlehem Hospital for the Criminally Insane, better known as Bedlam Hospital, in London and then eventually transferred to Pentonville Prison, also in the capital.

Despite escaping the hangman, Townley's guilt preyed heavy on his mind. On 12 February 1865, he attended chapel at Pentonville Prison where he sung part of the hymn *Abide With Me*. Following his religious devotions he left the chapel and jumped off a parapet, killing himself.

CHAPTER 25

Death After a Funeral: The Fiery Death of John McMorrow 1864

John McMorrow, a sixty-four-year-old miner, had attended a funeral with his forty-eight-year-old wife Mary on 24 June 1864, but little would anyone have known that there would be another death so soon after the conclusion of the service.

The couple had both consumed a large amount of alcohol throughout the majority of the course of the day and at 1am John was very drunk and was sleeping on a sofa by the fireplace at their home in North Wingfield. At 2am, however, he woke up with a start to discover that he was on fire, with his waistcoat and trousers already burnt by the flames. He called for help but saw his wife running away, allegedly laughing.

Mrs Garrick, who also lived in the house, was told, 'I have cooked his goose at last,' by the hysterical wife.

The flames were extinguished and there was hope the man's life had been saved. McMorrow was badly injured but the following day he was able to tell the police that he had been burnt by Mary McMorrow. She naturally denied the allegation but the crime became one of murder when John later died as a result of his burns.

There were doubts about John's statement, when other lodgers in the house claimed that McMorrow had told them it was not his wife who had burnt him, but the evidence of Garrick and the victim himself, was considered to be sufficiently damning. At the inquest on 16 July 1864, the jury found her guilty of killing John but did not believe there had been malicious intent. Accordingly, they returned a verdict of manslaughter.

At Mary's trial in 1865 she was convicted of manslaughter and sentenced to seven years of penal servitude at Parkhurst women's prison on the Isle of Wight. She was considered to be a very well behaved prisoner but her time of incarceration was relatively short lived; she died on 9 September 1866 with 'distortion of the spine'.

CHAPTER 26

An Unhappy Union:
The Murder of Harriet Wager
by her Husband
1866

In 1866, Edward Wager's violent temper finally resulted in him fulfilling the fears of many of those who had been close to him. He was a vicious man who thought little, if anything, of raising his fists to anyone; a habit that had earned him a place in a prison cell on several occasions. He had been married twice by the time he was thirty-seven, his first wife having divorced him on account of his cruelty towards her. His second wife, however, was not so lucky.

After his divorce he had met Harriet, who was a widow, and they quickly acquainted themselves with one another, resulting in an unhappy marriage. According to press reports this unhappy and fatal union had taken place only two months before she was murdered. The relationship characteristically saw several incidents of violence in the short time, culminating in her being beaten and drowned.

It was Christmas Eve in 1866 that Wager returned home from Hassop where he had been drinking, to Bleaklow Farm, Calver, where he lived with his wife as a tenant farmer. There he had tea with Harriet and a friend named Alice Hancock who had been present upon his arrival. After tea there was some argument, which Wager described at the inquest into his wife's death as being a 'little nonsense', which caused offence to his wife and she went off, declaring she could not stand to be there any longer. The little nonsense was an early stage in a sequence of events which saw Wager wake up in Bakewell lock-up on Christmas Day.

In his account before the coroner, Wager claimed he went after his wife but could not see where she went. He eventually found her, at a wall close to the stackyard where, he alleged, his wife threatened to commit suicide out of jealousy over her husband's behaviour with Hancock. According to his story she told him, 'I have seen plenty. I am quite satisfied. I will make away with myself before I will stand this work.' His account of events continued with his alleged instructions to his wife to come back inside. 'Don't be foolish,' he claimed to have said, 'come into the house. Alice Hancock will stay all night and we can have a game of cards.' After some persuasion, and no doubt with reluctance if the story had any truth, Harriet went back to the house and he kissed her before telling her not to be foolish again because what he had done had only 'been done in nonsense'.

Wager then claimed he asked his wife to hail 'little Ben', Harriet's son, who was down in one of the fields, because he wanted the boy to tie up some 'strange beasts' which he had just bought, which had never been tied up before. The boy was called for but did not come, so Harriet allegedly went after him. Hancock went to the door and saw that Harriet was saying something from a distance which she could not hear. Hancock went home at this time and Wager went after his wife. Harriet had only minutes left to live.

Naturally Wager denied having committed murder. Instead he claimed to have found his wife climbing over a wall into the 'deep rake', a feature of the local lead mining. When he approached he saw her under a rock with her mouth bleeding, according to his account. She then allegedly started to walk towards the house and when asked what she was doing she jumped into the Bleaklow Dam whilst she was 'more than a dozen yards' in front of him.

According to Wager he saw two lead miners, Richard Sellers and his son Roger, walk past but they took no notice of his cries for help. They gave evidence that they saw Wager chasing after Harriet and watched him as he beat her, but they accepted neither had intervened. Wager then called for Hancock but she did not come although he thought she was nearby, which she was not.

Allegedly fearing his wife would drown he took off his shoes but when he tried to jump into the dam he could not do so because he had no courage, having never seen anyone drown before, so instead he stood on the bank for a few minutes 'fretting'. He claimed he wished he had jumped in and drowned himself. Irrespective of his alleged thoughts, Wager made no effort to raise the alarm that his wife was in the water. It was William Goddard who found the body and alerted Inspector Cruit from Stoney Middleton. Wager had fled by this time.

It is not terribly surprising that the jury at Wager's trial on 6 March 1867, who presumably did not know anything of his previous criminal record, found the defendant's explanation for how his wife had died, and the defence's case as a whole, difficult to accept. They had heard additional evidence from Dr Wrench whose post-mortem examination had shown Harriet had suffered serious lacerations to the liver and other injuries, including broken bones in her mouth, indicating she had been violently beaten at some time shortly before her death. These injuries would have killed her within hours if she had not drowned, it was believed.

The jury returned a verdict of guilty on a charge of murder. Wager was sentenced to death but for unknown reasons he was more fortunate than most convicted murderers of his time. Instead of being hanged or being sentenced to a lifetime in prison, Wager found himself in a British prison for only six or seven months before boarding the *Hougoumont* for a historic journey, bound for Western Australia where he was sentenced to spend the remainder of his life. This was the only instance of

The *Hougoumont*, the ship which carried the final convicts to be transported to Australia, amongst whom was Derbyshire killer Edward Wager. Author's collection

a convicted murderer from Derbyshire having been 'trans-ported' during the nineteenth century.

The three-masted, full-rigged ship departed from London on 30 September before sailing along the southern coast to Portland, where it departed on 12 October, heading to the other side of the world. On board were 280 convicts and more than one hundred passengers consisting of prison guards and their families. The voyage to Australia lasted eighty-nine days, during which one of the prisoners died but otherwise the journey was fairly un-eventful. The ship arrived at Fremantle in Western Australia on 9 January 1868 and it proved to be the last ship to transport prisoners to the colony. Wager did indeed spend the remainder of his life in Australia, dying there eighteen years after his arrival.

CHAPTER 27

The Unsolved Murder of Sarah Footit 1867

Today they appear to be a presentable row of houses and it is hard to believe that the Midland Terrace, opposite the railway station in Derby, could have been the scene of a horrific murder more than 140 years ago.

It was in one of those houses that Sarah Footit, the fifty-nine-year-old widow of James Footit, a Derby solicitor, lived with her sons. On 25 July 1867, she had been in good health when one of her sons left her shortly before 1pm, having had lunch with her, but tragedy was to strike less than two hours later.

A friend called Harriet Williams visited the property at approximately 3.20 or 3.25pm but when she knocked on the

Cottages across from Derby railway station where Sarah Footit was brutally murdered. The author

front door there was no answer and it was found to be locked. She went to the back door and again there was no answer, which she thought was unusual. The back door was unlocked, however, so she entered the house. She was met with the gruesome sight of her friend laying unconscious on the sofa with a large blood clot on her head and blood on the sofa. She called for Mr Kennington, who lived next door, and his wife came in.

A surgeon, Mr Lindley, was sent for but there was little hope for the severely injured woman. At some point in time in the presence of the surgeon, Footit had been conscious, but when she was given brandy and water she was unable to drink it and vomited. Her right eye was dilated and she had a slow pulse. The best of efforts failed to prolong her life and she died at 9am on the following day. A post-mortem examination later revealed that she had died as a result of being struck on the head with a blunt instrument such as a hammer.

The son, James Arthur Footit, had returned home at about 3.35pm, having been sent for by a Mrs Richards. He believed that a number of pans were not in their usual places, which he thought to be odd, but Harriet Williams thought her friend must have cleaned up after dinner.

There were no signs of disturbance or of a struggle, suggesting the killer caught his or her victim unaware and acted with speed and possibly that Footit knew her attacker. It is curious that the front door was locked, which was not usually the case. Perhaps the killer locked the door and wished to prolong the discovery of the crime or wished to prevent anyone from disturbing the perpetration of it.

There were valuable pieces of silver on the sideboard but nothing was seemingly missing from the house. A box of money on the table contained two half crowns and a shilling piece and there were a number of silver spoons on the table. A second son, Henry, did not think his mother had any more money or valuable belongings to those accounted for. The police concluded that a vagabond had intended to steal but was disturbed and panicked killing the widow before fleeing empty-handed. Did Williams disturb the killer? Did he panic? Perhaps robbery was not the motive at all. No murder weapon was found and all of the hammers and hatchets belonging to the house were accounted for. If the killer had taken a weapon it would imply he had entered the building anticipating the possibility of violence.

The building could have been accessed without neighbours seeing. It was concluded there might not have been a scream, with a state of unconsciousness having been instantaneous. However, James noticed that there was a graze on his mother's left hand which he had not noticed earlier that day, which suggested to him that she had tried to defend herself. If this was the case the attack must still have been swiftly carried out but it increased the likelihood that the victim knew her attacker or that she was caught entirely by surprise, with any struggle being minimal.

An inquest before Mr Whiston found that this was the case of 'wilfull murder against some person or persons unknown'. The coroner, for reasons that we may never know, disagreed with the jury's verdict but it was recorded nonetheless. Perhaps he had suspicions as to who was responsible, based on the evidence presented before him, but if he did there was never any firm evidence to make any arrests or bring about any convictions for the murder of Mrs Footit which disappeared into the annals of criminal history as yet another unsolved murder.

CHAPTER 28

Tragedy on the Farm: Murder and Suicide at Stoney Houghton 1868

Often the cause of a murder seems so frightfully absurd that it is hard to reconcile the consequences with the motive or motives that led to them. This was the case in a murder and suicide at Stoney Houghton, near Pleasley, on 2 April 1868.

At about 5am that morning a well-to-do farmer named John Wass, who had farmed almost 200 acres of land for more than thirty years, argued with one of his workers, Robert Brown, who was nineteen years old, regarding his horses. There had been great animosity between the two men, both of whom were described as having fiery tempers. Just two months earlier Wass had assaulted the teenager with a three-pronged fork and was summoned before the magistrates. There was a reconciliation and Brown dropped the charges. However, any hopes of a long lasting good work relationship between employee and employer were not to be realised. Following his lucky escape from the law, Wass' temper increased further and he became more despondent. Brown should have taken his opportunity to leave Wass' employment but for the want of what was probably a poorly paid job he remained working for a man who posed a danger to him.

On that fateful April morning, Wass had called Brown shortly after rising at 5am. However, he became infuriated when Brown failed to arrive until approximately an hour later. When Brown finally went to his boss, after 6am, he gave an insolent response to why he was late. This immediately angered Wass who went to the house to fetch his gun. He approached Brown as the teenager stood on the road fronting the house, and pointed the weapon towards the worker's back. Pulling the trigger, a loud shot rang out and Brown fell to the ground, dying instantaneously, the full shot having hit him in the back, shattering his spine.

The sister of Wass' wife, Mary or Sarah Wilson (press reports gave differing first names), heard the shot and immediately ran outside to see what had happened and saw the dead man on the ground. She hailed a youth who was nearby and instructed him to run to Glapwell and fetch a police officer.

Upon seeing what he had done as the result of his rash actions, and having heard that a police presence had been requested, Wass rushed to the house, entered one of the downstairs room where he reloaded his weapon and took it upstairs.

It was whilst Police Constable Hanson was on his way to the farm that Wass placed the end of the barrel of the weapon in his mouth. A local man, James Meakin, ran to the room and tried to get to the killer when the gun was fired a second time. Wass had shot himself through the head, 'blowing off the top of the brain pan'. There was no hope of him surviving. The policeman soon arrived, as did a large number of sightseers who wanted to view the scene of such a tragedy.

CHAPTER 29

'Johnny Has Gone to Heaven': The Killing of John William Ingham 1869

Many parents have, during times of desperation, resorted to killing their offspring, and usually themselves, in order to lessen the financial burdens or to end the family's suffering. Indeed in the days before the Welfare State and during times of large-scale unemployment and exploitation of those fortunate to secure short term work, murderous and suicidal thoughts were much more prevalent than in our own time. Given the choice of an early and painful death through malnutrition, a lifetime in the workhouse, or what was thought to be a relatively dignified death in the control of the parent it is not overly surprising that some parents, driven by desperation and an entire lack of hope, chose the option of killing their children and themselves to bring to an end what must have been a terrible suffering. And so criminal history is filled with such instances of families being murdered during times of chronic poverty where one or both parents have had their minds afflicted by homicidal thoughts.

Whether it was for this reason that Annie Ingham killed her youngest child, having previously expressed an intention to also kill herself, is uncertain but it would certainly seem to have been a factor in causing the tragedy.

George Wiggin Ingham probably had little reason to worry when he went to work on 26 April 1869. He was employed as a porter at the Midland Railway Station, living in nearby Barrow Street, in the Litchurch area of Derby, with his wife Annie, a twenty-seven-year-old needlewoman, whom he had been married to for approximately four years. The couple had two children: two boys, the oldest aged three years and the youngest, named John William, who was nine months old. When he went to work that Monday morning George left his wife and the youngest child in bed, with the older boy lying in a cot in the same room.

It was known Annie had suffered from some form of depression, but her husband would have had little understanding of the nature of his wife's illness and probably did not fully appreciate the threat she posed, but he would quickly learn she was very much a danger. He would later describe her as having been in a 'low desponding way for about four months' prior to that tragic day but had hoped she could just 'shake off' her psychiatric problems. Annie had complained of a constant great pain in the top of her head and was said to be in poor health and 'low spirited'. She was also often heard to speak incoherently. In February of that year, her doctor, Francis, had said that knives and other such objects should be kept away from her because he was concerned she might want to kill herself. On one occasion she had disappeared in the morning and returned home later in the day, very upset, saying that she had been to Chellaston to try and drown herself, a task she would have carried out, she claimed, had her child not cried and disturbed her suicidal thoughts. On another occasion she had asked for poison so that she could kill herself. There had been no concern that she could harm anyone but herself, however, but this was certainly not an illness that could simply be shaken off.

Before George left for work, according to his later testimony at the inquest held that same day at Mr Baldock's Arboretum Hotel

An article from the *Derby Mercury* on 27 April 1869 regarding the murder of John Ingram. Author's collection in Litchurch, he had a conversation with his wife after she woke him up in order that he should go to work. She told him, 'Look at this child. Is he not a sweet little thing?' She asked him to kiss her and they discussed her health. 'Well, are you going to be better today?' he asked before adding, 'You must shake off that feeling you have for the sake of those little things that are lying here.' He was referring to the baby and the older child lying in the cot nearby.

At some point in time between 7 and 8am on that April morning, after George had left for work, Annie got up and found her husband's razor, which was laying on the dressing table and which George had either forgotten to hide or had not realised the importance of preventing his wife from taking hold of. It was not with the intention of suicide, however, that led Annie to seize the blade. She instead decided to cut the throat of her youngest child, killing it instantly in the opinion of those who examined the body. She had not inflicted any injuries on the other boy or herself.

Having killed her youngest son, Annie went downstairs, left her house and went next door to the home of Evelyn Hallam. When Hallam answered the door she saw the killer who announced, 'I've done it,' before adding she had 'Done for Johnny.' It may have been difficult to believe from her manner that she had just killed her own baby, for she seemed to be calm, if it had not been for the blood that covered her hands which she held up to the surprised neighbour to prove her action. 'You have not murdered him?' Hallam asked. 'Yes I have,' she replied.

Hallam called for Annie's sister, Elizabeth Law, who normally lived with the Inghams. To her sister, Annie again repeated her confession, telling her, 'Johnny has gone to heaven. I have done it. I have sent him to heaven.' The women ran upstairs and found the baby, which was clearly dead, with the razor on the dressing table covered in blood.

When he arrived, Superintendent Whieldon took Annie Ingham into custody on suspicion of murder and Hallam went to fetch George Ingham. George was sent for within approximately fifteen minutes of his arrival at work, such was the speed at which events had taken place. Upon arriving home George asked his wife, 'Annie, what is amiss?' If he had already not been told that his son was dead, and even if he did know, he would have been shocked by her response and the manner in which it was delivered: 'I have done it. I have done it. I have sent Johnny to heaven.' He ran upstairs and saw his son lying on the bed covered in blood.

The family was reasonably well off but for some time prior to the incident Annie had constantly feared that they would end up in poverty. Five days before the baby was killed, Annie had told a neighbour that she believed Johnny was going to come into 'want'. This fear, fuelled by her mental illness, was quite possibly why she killed her child. Nonetheless, at the inquest the jury dismissed the claims of insanity and found that the child had died as a result of wilful murder.

However, at her trial in July 1869, during which she had been so affected after pleading 'not guilty' to murder that she required a seat in the dock, the judge, Baron Cleasby, accepted that she had suffered from insanity, his opinion based on her medical history. He directed the jury to acquit on the charge of murder on the grounds of insanity which, after a minute or so of deliberations, they agreed to do. It was quite possibly the correct verdict. It would appear to be quite likely that Annie was suffering from post-natal depression, a disorder unknown during the Victorian period. She was detained at Her Majesty's pleasure and had to be assisted out of the court.

CHAPTER 30

A Crime of Horrifying Brutality: The Murder of Matilda Hitchcock 1869

On the morning of Tuesday 2 November 1869, at Farnah Green, a mile from Belper, to the west of the town, William Hitchcock, a forty-seven-year-old stone-cutter, set off to town. Whatever his plans were for the day, if they extended beyond his usual session of ale drinking, is unknown but they ended in one of the most horrifyingly brutal murders to take place in Victorian Derbyshire.

Hitchcock had gone to the town on his own but later in the day his wife, Matilda, who was forty-five years old, also went to Belper with the two children where they met Hitchcock. At about 5.30pm Hitchcock and his wife started heading in the direction of home. Where the children were at this point in time is unclear. Upon seeing the Georgia Vaults in Bridge Street, Belper, Hitchcock went in for a drink leaving his wife outside. He was refused service on account of being known to be violent whilst under the influence of alcohol, and left the premises cursing. From there he continued with his wife over Belper Bridge and turned into the meadows which had a path leading towards Farnah Green, passing the place which would later be the home of the James Bond actor Timothy Dalton, a century later. What precisely happened next is unknown but even if Matilda had played any provocative role it did not justify any level of violence against her, and certainly not the level that was witnessed by a number of shocked onlookers.

A Mrs Garratt was walking through the meadows when she saw Hitchcock battering his wife with an umbrella. It appeared

Bridge Street, Belper, along which William Hitchcock and his wife walked on their way to Farnah Green and where Hitchcock tried to become further intoxicated. The author

Matilda had wanted to rest through tiredness of walking but her husband would not let her. A Mrs Wood then walked past and saw Hitchcock kicking his wife. Mrs Garrett walked off towards Belper. A Mrs Payne walked along and heard the wife shouting, 'Oh cossey don't murder me. Oh don't take my life.' None of these women intervened, perhaps through fear. If they had, Matilda's life might possibly have been saved.

Two more women came along heading towards Windley, a few miles south west of Farnah Green. They saw Hitchcock standing over his wife. She was clearly seriously injured and the two women told Hitchcock she was dying and that he should take her home. Her suffering was far from over; upon being given this advice Hitchcock picked her up and dragged her behind him for nearly half a mile. The women followed and went into the house where they were able to examine her injuries more closely. Matilda's face was covered in blood, apparently from head to toe. Her head had been viciously battered with one of her eyes knocked out of its socket.

Farnah Green, near Belper, where William Hitchock brutally attacked his wife in 1869. The author

Indeed, at the inquest into Matilda's death Mr Thomas Johnson, a surgeon, said that the head, face and neck were severely swollen and discoloured, especially both temples, with major bruising on the left hip, a distinct bruise on the right thigh, lots of bleeding under the scalp, considerable blood around the left eye, a large amount of bleeding on the left side of the brain and a small quantity on the right side of the brain. It was the bleeding to the brain which had caused death, in the surgeon's opinion. Further, the left big toe and nail were torn off as a result of her being dragged along the ground whilst dying.

Yet despite such violence and ill treatment during her carriage to her home, there were still weak but evident signs of life when the women examined her. She was conscious but never spoke. It is said that as soon as the women left, Hitchcock went to The Bell public house (now probably the Blue Bell Inn) and drank until 11pm. While their father was out drinking, the two children returned home to find their dying mother on the floor. They managed to get her to bed and called the surgeon,

Mr Johnson, but medical intervention could only prolong life for a short time. She died at 5am on 5 November. Whether or not an earlier medical intervention could have altered the outcome is academic, but given the nature of the injuries it would seem unlikely that she would have had any hope of survival.

Superintendent Shaw apprehended Hitchcock on the Wednesday night as he was drinking and arrested him for assault. He was then taken to Belper Police station. Belper's first police station was built in 1848 and housed the County Headquarters between 1857 and 1859. It ceased to be a police station in the 1960s. The following day, when the detective told the killer of his wife's death, after he had sobered up, Hitchcock apparently laughed. His apparent lack of remorse was further demonstrated when it was said that on the previous day, when one of the Windley women told him Matilda was going to die, he had replied, 'I am afraid not. She has been a trouble to me a long time.'

It would have been an open and shut case with witnesses having seen the crime being perpetrated and with such ferocity

Belper's first police station which was in use between 1848 and the 1960s, where William Hitchcock was questioned over his wife's murder and where he committed suicide. The author

it would no doubt have led to crowds of angry people from across the county descending upon the court and the place of lawful execution. Yet there was to be no trial and his execution was witnessed by no one, for Hitchcock's hangman was none other than himself. On the evening he found himself charged with murder officers looked into his cell and found him hanging with his handkerchief round his neck, tied to one of the bars. He was dead and, in the opinion of many, had avoided justice with the full truth of what had happened and why, never being revealed at trial, if indeed the killer would have ever explained his actions. The jury at the inquest into Matilda's death found that it was a case of wilful murder committed by William Hitchcock.

CHAPTER 31

Murder or Provoked Suicide? The Controversial Death of Mary Ann Winfield 1871

A woman lost her life following years of brutal ill treatment at the hands of her husband but the circumstances surrounding her death are as much a mystery today as they were in March 1871 when her body was found in the River Derwent in Derby.

Mary Ann Winfield, a woman aged about thirty-five to forty, lived with her husband, William, a pot hawker, at their lodgings at 31 Erasmus Street, which was bounded by the canal and the Derwent. On Saturday 4 March 1871, the couple drank together at The Wilmot Arms in Castle Street and left shortly before midnight. According to Ann Stratham, the wife of the landlord, she was not sure whether the couple were drunk, although she was only too aware that they had been drinking for some time. It would appear that Winfield's demeanour had at least somewhat been affected by drink. The night had already seen arguments and violence to which Mary had become accustomed but this time it was to end in tragedy.

After leaving The Wilmot Arms, the couple passed Siddall's Lane and walked across the Morledge, to begin walking over a lengthy wooden bridge over the Derwent. A man, who from his house had a view of the bridge, said that at about midnight, when he was going to bed, he heard a row and saw Mary being struck between the shoulders causing her to stagger, although she kept on her feet. Winfield then began to speak more kindly to his wife, according to the witness, although he could not hear exactly what was said. The witness then retired for the night and saw and heard nothing more of relevance.

Thomas Garrett, who was approximately fifteen yards away from the quarrelling pair, also saw Mary being struck heavily on the back, which was followed by her exclamation of 'Oh don't!' She stumbled but did not fall and the argument continued. George Upton saw the incident but was uncertain whether he saw one or two blows being inflicted. William Calladine, a watchman at Messrs Pegg & Harper's colour works in the Morledge, saw an argument, whilst he was on the towpath at a distance of approximately forty yards.

Witnesses later spoke of a loud altercation as the couple were midway across the bridge, but no one intervened, believing it to be best left between man and wife. Even when witnesses saw Winfield strike his wife several times in her lower body they just watched and walked on. Mary screamed and still they did nothing.

William Shepherd was next to see something that would be of importance. As he walked past Exeter Street at quarter past midnight he heard loud screams and when he reached the top of the canal bridge he saw Winfield running away. When asked what was the matter, Winfield ignored the man. Shepherd saw Winfield again, approximately five minutes later, at Erasmus Street and was told Mary had jumped over the bridge into the water. Shepherd would later tell the police and the inquest into Mary's death that since her brother's death Mary had become quarrelsome, although it is clear that the main instigator of any argument and violence that night was Winfield and not his grieving wife.

Shortly after midnight, and after Winfield had first seen Shepherd, Mr Henchley was disturbed by loud knocking at his door. 'Be quick!' the visitor shouted as he banged on the door. Henchley opened the door to find Winfield looking distressed. 'There's a woman in the water,' the late visitor exclaimed. 'Have you the drags at hand?' Perhaps in disbelief, especially given Winfield's relatively calm demeanour which quickly replaced the initial urgency in his actions, Henchley asked if Winfield had said there was indeed a woman in the water. 'Yes I did,' was the reply, 'It is my wife.'

Henchley went to fetch the drags, receiving no assistance from Winfield who said, 'I believe she has gone, poor soul. I am sure she has gone.' He then left and went home.

Despite the several witnesses who saw or heard the altercation, no one saw Mary jump over, or be thrown over the
3ft-high railings at the bridge. The reports of violent behaviour,
however, inevitably resulted in an arrest. Inspector Fearn and
Detective Spibey arrested Winfield on the Monday morning
at his lodgings. He did himself no favours when denying to the
inspector that there had been any argument. 'We never had a
word,' the suspect said before explaining his version of events:

> We went marketing on the Saturday night, and afterwards
> went to Willow-row and to a public house and when we got
> on the Long Bridge she said 'I'm jealous' and immediately
> threw herself over the bridge.

He claimed he had grabbed his wife's wrist but had lost his grip.

It was not difficult to see that the police were convinced
Winfield was lying and that he had killed his wife, whose body
was recovered from the water on the Sunday about noon. The
fact he had not told Shepherd that his wife was in the water,
when he first encountered him suggested to the police that it

The Derwent close to Derby railway station, near to where Mary Ann
Winfield drowned after jumping or being pushed from a bridge. The author

was not an accident. A post mortem revealed abrasions consistent with a fall. However, it was never disputed she had been physically assaulted and the injuries that are present on someone who falls into a river from a height are in many ways the same as those present on the body of someone who is pushed.

The coroner at the inquest disagreed and told the jury that there were strong suspicions but they did not amount to anything more than that. The jury concurred and returned an open verdict, merely recording that Mary was 'found drowned'. Winfield was never brought to trial.

Was this a case of murder with pre-meditated intent? Was it a suicide or an accident whereby, fuelled by anger and alcohol, in a few moments of madness Winfield had pushed his wife over the bridge and almost immediately regretted his action? The evidence seems rather compelling to assume that, regardless of the answer, Mary Ann Winfield lost her life as a consequence of the prolonged abuse she suffered at the hands of her husband, whether he killed her or she ended her own life to escape his cruelty.

An article from the *Derby Mercury* on 7 March 1871 regarding the then suspected murder of Mary Ann Winfield. Author's collection

SHOCKING MURDER AT DERBY

A shocking and cool-blooded wife murder has just occurred at Derby. A pot-hawker, named William Winfield, a middle-aged man, had lately entered the town, and had taken lodgings at a house in Erasmus Street, which is a central place, and on one side bounded by a canal and the River Derwent. The victim of the murder is Mary Ann Winfield, about thirty-five or forty years of age, his wife. It would appear that the parties had lived very unhappily together for many years past, and on many occasions the husband had been known to brutally ill-treat her. On Saturday evening they had been drinking together at the Wilmot Arms public-house, in Castle Street, and left there a little before midnight on their way to the lodging-house in Erasmus Street. On the way thither they passed along Siddall's Lane, across the Morledge, and then had occasion to pass over a lengthy wooden bridge, extending right across the basin of the River Derwent, known in the town as the "Long Bridge." Several people met them as they were proceeding along, and each of those persons heard a loud alteration between the man and his wife. The language used by the husband was of an abusive and threatening character. As they were about mid-way on the bridge one or more persons saw them "close together." The man was afterwards seen to strike the woman in the lower part of the body several times, and what followed, of course, remains a mystery. A slight scream was heard, but the people who were just crossing at the time were impressed that it was merely a dispute between the man and his wife, and accordingly proceeded on about their business. It is suggested that the man then threw his wife over the bridge, for in overtaking other people at the end of the bridge, he never complained that his wife was in the river, and no information was given of the occurrence for a considerable time afterwards. Going to the Police Office early on Sunday morning, the man said his wife had drowned herself, and he believed she was below the weir. They had had some words together, he added, and she threw herself over the bridge, saying she was jealous of him. The statement he made was that she got over the bridge, and he caught hold of her wrist in time to keep her from dropping into the river; but, as no one came to his assistance, his strength failed him, and she fell into the basin. This account is in complete contradiction to that made by several other people who were known to have gone over the bridge at the time. A search was made for the body, and it was discovered on Sunday, at noon, many hundred yards below the weir. Detective-inspector Fearn, accompanied by Detective Spibey, proceeded to the lodgings of the man on Sunday morning, and there apprehended him on a charge of murder. In reply he said she was jealous of him, and threw herself into the river.

CHAPTER 32

Killed for a Sixpence: The Death of William Eyre 1874

An alcohol-fuelled fight regarding the ownership of a sixpence ended in tragedy one Saturday evening in July 1874. On the fatal night, Snowden Topham, a twenty-six or thirty-two-year-old (press articles gave varying ages) fitter from Albion Street and William Eyre, a shoemaker from Friar Gate, were sat indoors at 1 Court, Orchard Street, possibly the same Orchard Street on which the newly-born baby was left dead fourteen years earlier. The scene of this crime, and indeed the whole of the small Orchard Street itself, has been developed upon in recent years. The property was owned by a man known as 'Whisket Shaw' whose real name was Frederick Shaw. Mary Shaw, who had lived with Topham for eight years, was also in the room as were Louisa Shaw, Sarah Mudford and two girls, one of whom was a fifteen-year-old named Martha Hickman. All of the adults were drinking.

As the evening progressed both Topham and Eyre had become 'very tipsy', according to Mudford and 'beastly intoxicated', according to Hickman. The two men had never before met and when asked by Topham who he was, Eyre had replied, 'I'll serve you as I have served many others if you ask who I am.' As it happened Eyre was to marry Shaw's sister, although there was no intention for the two men to make pleasant acquaintances.

At about 9pm Topham told his companions that he was going to go and by a quart of ale. With this in mind one of the men took sixpence from his pocket but the coin slipped out of his hand and fell to the floor. Eyre picked up the coin and declared that it was his, calling Topham a liar for saying it belonged to him. A fight followed between the two men for ownership of the money. Hickman had seen Topham produce the coin half an hour before Eyre arrived at the house, suggesting it did belong to him. Mary Shaw offered to pay the sixpence out of her own money rather than witness any fight. At this time Mudford left the room but before she did so she noticed that Eyre had given Topham the money. Mary Shaw had told him 'No Bill, give it him. You know it's not yours. It's Snowden's.' Eyre had reluctantly handed it over saying that if it was his he ought to keep it. His words were, 'God strike me dead if it is yours.' For her efforts of trying to prevent any violence, Mary Shaw was hit in the eye by the back of Topham's hand. Angered by this, Eyre told the brute that he would rather die than strike a woman. His words were to be proven to be unfortunately chosen.

Topham may have been given the money but the issue was still in contention. The fight became increasingly violent with Eyre punching Topham in the face, causing his head to go through a window. Mudford later recalled hearing a smash of glass and a woman shouting 'It's poor Bill's head!' However, worse was to follow and having had his head pushed through a window, Topham was determined to cause greater harm to his opponent. Eyre had Topham by the throat with his left hand and was hitting him with his right. Mary Shaw, undeterred by having been struck, pulled Eyre away from Topham and was hit in the chest by Eyre, although seemingly by accident. Eventually Eyre exclaimed, 'I am done for,' or 'I'm bleeding,' along with more colourful language, and it was seen that there was a large amount of blood pouring down his legs. Eyre staggered out of the building and went to the front of the house informing Mudford, 'Snowden has stabbed me,' and 'I am ripped up.' He asked another neighbour, Samuel Peatson, to fetch a doctor. Mudford took Eyre into her home, which was a neighbouring property, and removed his trousers to try and treat the wound which was found to be in the man's groin. Only one minute later he was dead.

Thomas Hill, a boilermaker, saw Topham walking away from the building immediately after he stabbed Eyre. Topham informed the man that he had killed Eyre and wanted to go to the privy. Hall claimed that whilst with the killer there he had been given a brief account of events leading up to the stabbing, which Topham alleged was 'the God's truth', including the fight over the sixpence. According to Hill's later testimony before the magistrates, Topham told him, 'Eyre then got up to strike me and I lifted up my knife and struck him.' He claimed to be sorry for what he had done and knew he would be hanged for it.

When arrested Topham admitted to Police Constable Barker that he had stabbed Eyre and said he had given away the knife, but he did not know who to. He claimed the death had been accidental, saying, 'I am sorry, and shall be hung. I had a knife in my hand when a quarrel commenced. Eyre gave me sixpence with one hand and struck me with the other. Eyre made a spring at me and I put up my hand, but I do not know how the wound was inflicted.' After being charged with murder, whilst in the house, Topham kissed Eyre's face. He was then taken into custody.

Mr Copestake later examined the body, which was positioned on a chair when the surgeon arrived. The wound was found to be approximately an inch in length and two and a half inches deep on the upper part of the left thigh. The floor around was covered in blood, with the large amount of blood loss being the result of the femoral vein and artery being partially severed. He also had a small cut above his left eyebrow, which may have been caused by a blunt instrument, possibly the back of the sofa. It was Copestake's opinion that it was possible that the thigh injury arose when Topham threw himself on top of Eyre whilst the deceased was sat down on the sofa holding his knife. He did not think Eyre could have been stood up whilst he received the injury, due to its position.

When examined by the magistrates before being committed for trial, Topham was described by the local press as 'remarkably self-possessed' and that he was indifferent to what was occurring. He denied murder, telling the magistrates, 'Oh I am innocent of the deed.'

The defence argued that Topham had been cutting tobacco with his knife as he sat on the sofa, when Eyre jumped upon him, and so Eyre acquired his fatal injury through accident rather than malice. Indeed, Topham was sat on the sofa and Eyre did throw himself upon him, but no witnesses recalled seeing Topham with his knife and tobacco at that moment in time. Mary Shaw had seen him with the knife a few minutes earlier, cutting either tobacco or his fingernails.

This defence argument was contradicted by Topham's own account immediately after the crime. Topham told a man he had stabbed Eyre although he had earlier told Louisa Shaw, who was upstairs when Eyre was stabbed, 'I've done nothing.' The man, Isaac Bingham, was told, 'I could not help it. He struck me in the eye and I let into him.' Bingham told the killer he should not move. Topham accepted he would have to stay until the police arrived, despite Mary Shaw pleading to him that they should flee, and added, 'I know if he dies I shall only have to be hung for it.' When the police arrived he asked, 'Am I going to be taken as a murderer?'

Topham was taken as a murderer and stood trial for that crime. However, his defence team were persuasive in their argument that there was no premeditation or malice. Topham was convicted of manslaughter.

The story did not end there. Convicted of manslaughter, Topham had been released by July 1881 and was living with Mary at Cavendish Buildings in Brook Street in Derby. In that month Mary Topham (Mary may have married Topham although it was not uncommon for female cohabitants to adopt their partner's surname during the late Victorian period) was charged with assaulting the killer. The police had been alerted by the cries of 'murder!' emanating from the building. When they investigated they found Snowden Topham bleeding heavily from a wound on his temple, inflicted by a cup. Mary explained her action by claiming she had been treated badly by Topham for a long time and that she had caught him with another woman. Unfortunately her punishment could not be discovered during research for this book but it would seem that despite time in prison, and his experience which could conceivably have resulted in his execution or lifetime imprisonment if it had not been for such a good legal team, Topham had not learnt to control his anger.

CHAPTER 33

An Unprovoked Atrocity:
The Murder of William Brown
1875

It was 9pm on 12 June 1875 that a cattle drover named Frederick Read was stood in a yard near his lodgings in Bag Lane (now called East Street), Derby, when he heard a loud cry of 'I'll kill you, you old ————.' Somewhat taken aback, Read looked through the window of the house from which the shout emanated, which happened to be the house next to his lodgings, and saw a woman striking an elderly man about the head with a piece of iron. Read immediately ran to his lodgings to request help from his landlady, Mrs Hannah Lindley. 'Go down the yard or they'll kill that old man,' he told her.

When Read and Lindley arrived they entered the building and saw the attacker, Rose Brown, a fifty-seven-year-old hawker, strike the elderly man two or three times more, but this time with her hand. It was clear she was intoxicated, unlike her victim. Again, Rose said she would kill the man and shouted abuse at him. 'She has done for me this time,' the old man was heard to say. Only at that time did they go to find a policeman.

The man was William Brown, Rose's husband. Remarkably, according to newspaper reports, he was ninety-eight years old at the time of the attack, although even if this was an overestimate (reports of age were not always accurate and often even an individual would not know how old they were, especially the more elderly members of Victorian society) his old age was clear to all. Despite his age and infirmity, which saw him walking doubled up, he still sold bootlaces in the Market Place. He was a 'quiet, inoffensive man', according to Lindley. The marriage had been an unhappy one, and there had been previous quarrels

East Street, Derby, known as Bag Lane in Victorian times, where Rose Brown murdered her elderly husband, William, in 1875. The author

during the three or four months that they had been living on Bag Lane. On one occasion Lindley had removed William from the property because his wife had cut his head badly. The couple had argued more seriously when the rent was due, as it was on the day of this tragedy.

When Read returned with Police Sergeant Adams, he found Brown was having his wounds bathed at Lindley's lodgings, having been moved there with the assistance of another resident, James Wilson, who had heard Rose's murderous threats. 'She was always on to him,' he would later recall. Whilst at the lodgings William remained conscious and managed to speak, saying he was in a bad way.

When questioned by Adams, Rose said she had done nothing to her husband, before eventually saying, 'What I have done, I have with this,' pointing to an iron poker.

William was taken to the infirmary and was still conscious when he arrived, which is remarkable given the extent of his injuries and his age. Adams returned from the hospital and charged Rose with cutting and wounding her husband.

She denied the offence of cutting, telling the policeman, 'I am innocent of cutting. What I have done I have done with a poker. I will die before I will own up to anything else. You may take me and hang me if you like.'

The poker was not identified by witnesses who had seen the attack as being the weapon used to inflict the injuries. However, no other weapon was found. The fact Rose denied cutting using any other object is of fairly minor importance given she freely admitted she was responsible for causing the injuries.

The injuries were serious contrary to how they were interpreted by the defence. Thomas Highton, the house surgeon at Derby Infirmary, informed the eventual trial of Rose Brown, in July 1875, that there were sixteen scalp wounds, all of which cut close to the skull. There was also a wound on the nose and contusions about the face, all caused by a sharp instrument and not, in his opinion, by a poker. He said, 'I think it is impossible for the poker produced to have inflicted the wounds.' The wounds in themselves were not necessarily life threatening, he believed, but that the cause of death had been Erysipalas, a form of blood poisoning, which had set in five days after the attack. This allowed the defence to argue it was not a case of murder.

Mr Buzzard, of the prosecution, told the jury that Rose had repeatedly admitted the crime but had claimed the weapon of choice was a poker because either it was or that she had used a more vicious weapon, a fact she wanted to conceal. He added that there could not have been provocation on the part of William because of his age and because he was infirm. He posed no threat to warrant the amount of violence inflicted upon him. Therefore, he argued, Rose Brown deliberately intended to kill her husband and the fact he died of an infection did not remove the fact that murder was the motive. The prosecution argued that had William Brown not been attacked he would not have died and therefore Rose Brown was guilty of murder.

An article from the *Derby Mercury* on 21 July 1875 regarding the murder of William Brown. Author's collection

Mr Wrightman, of the defence, countered this argument by suggesting his client did not have sufficient motive to kill William and that if she had intended to commit murder she was more than capable of doing so. He used the surgeon's evidence that the wounds were not severe as proof of his claim. Surely, however, this is not the case at all. She carried out a sustained physical attack, voicing her intention to commit murder, and the elderly man's life was only temporarily saved because she was interrupted in pursuing her task. It was also argued by the defence that the crime was committed as a result of alcohol and that Rose was not aware of her actions. She had said, 'I am guilty of striking him but I did not mean to kill him.'

The judge, Mr Justice Lindley, who was presumably not a relative of the prosecution witness, told the jury that there was no evidence for manslaughter because there had been no provocation. After a deliberation of only a few minutes the jury returned a verdict that Rose was guilty of murder but requested she be granted mercy on the grounds of her age; mercy she was unwilling to give her significantly older husband.

The verdict left no apparent impression on the murderer and she continued to show no remorse. Indeed whilst on the way to prison following her conviction she unbelievably said, 'I didn't kill the old man. I didn't. He killed himself.'

Sentencing her to death, Mr Justice Lindley told Rose that she should have treated her inoffensive elderly husband very differently and that it was clear she was guilty of such a wicked crime and all of the evidence supported that conclusion. Brown managed to escape the hangman's noose, with her death sentence being commuted to one of penal servitude for life.

CHAPTER 34

A Very Wicked Deed:
Murder and Suicide in Derby
1877

A 'fearful quarrel' between a man and his wife, during which his wife expressed a heat of the moment desire that she would rather be dead, resulted in a gruesome murder and suicide in Derby.

Shortly after 2pm, on Monday 12 February 1877, Jane Elizabeth Hicking was found murdered at the home which she shared with her husband, Samuel, a general dealer who traded at Sadler Gate. The couple lived in an upper room of a house in Irongate, Derby, above a butcher's shop. There is no evidence relating to how happy or unhappy the couple's marriage had been but certainly on 11 February there had been cause for great disagreement.

Hicking sent two letters on the Monday, which offered a partial explanation for what had taken place, in the form of a confession. Hicking was seen to post one of the letters, to his solicitor, with a second letter written to his brother. The letter to the solicitor read:

Dear Thomas,

I have committed a very wicked deed by killing my dear wife Jenny, and am going to commit suicide myself by hanging. I expect in the loft over Cooper's. The cause is we had a fearful quarrel last night, when we got back from a walk. We got to high words, and almost to blows. She said she wished she was dead, and I said I was, and the sooner we were gone the better. I could not sleep, and was brooding over it all night until half-past five this morning, and Jenny was asleep, and I bethought myself of some acid that was in the house, and I thought I would give it her, and then shoot myself, but when I attempted it she got up, and did not take it. So she ran to the door, and I followed her with a pistol, which I had loaded for to take my own life. It was loaded with two bullets, but it did not finish her, so then I cut her in the neck, and she was soon gone. I have written to my brother William, at Nottingham, and I should think he will soon be here. So I will conclude, hoping you will see after mine, and his, and their interests. I have been nearly off my head lately about money matters. If you get my letter before William arrive, which I expect will be about four o'clock, you will know what to do.

Yours unfortunately, S. Hicking.

Irongate, facing towards the Cathedral, painted by Louise Raynor in 1865.
Author's collection

Upon receiving the letter, the solicitor contacted the police and Superintendent McTurnan and Detective Sergeant Spibey broke down the door and found the terrible scene. Dr Gisborne was sent for and pronounced Jane dead, believing that she had probably been killed the previous night, contrary to what was said in Hicking's letter. Her throat had been viciously cut. She was naked but had been covered by bedclothes. Such was the force which her husband had used, that Jane's head had nearly been severed from her body. Her windpipe had been entirely cut and it was thought that death would have been instantaneous. A pistol was found on the floor, and a gunshot had been heard at 6am that morning, but there was no evidence that anyone had been wounded by this weapon although reports conflicted on this aspect of the case.

An article from the *Derby Mercury* regarding the murder of Hicking's wife prior to his own death. Author's collection

HORRIBLE WIFE MURDER IN DERBY.
ATTEMPTED SUICIDE OF THE MURDERER.

Soon after two o'clock yesterday afternoon, a tragedy of a horrible nature was discovered to have taken place in Derby. A man named Hicking, a general dealer, trading in Sadler gate,. occupied, with his wife, the upper storey of a house in Iron gate. The shop below is occupied by Mr. S. Smith, pork butcher. Hicking's solicitor received a letter from him by the mid-day post, informing him that he had murdered his wife, and that it was his intention to destroy himself. The solicitor at once communicated with the police, and Superintendent M'Ternan and Detective-sergeant Spibey went to the house. On breaking open the door of the room a terrible scene presented itself. Both Mr. and Mrs. Hicking lay on the floor in a pool of blood. The woman was undressed, but had her clothing thrown over her. Her head was nearly severed from her body. The windpipe was completely cut through, and death must have taken place immediately after the wound was inflicted. The man lay with his head on his wife's knee. He had a terrible gash in his throat, the windpipe being cut through. Superintendent M'Ternan at once went for Dr. Gisborne, and he, on arrival, at once pronounced the woman dead. He attended to the man's injuries, after which he was conveyed to the Infirmary. His injuries are of such a character that only slight hope is entertained of his recovery. From the appearance of the woman it is very probable that she was murdered during Sunday night. A pistol and some caps were found lying by the bodies, and the occupants of a neighbouring house heard the report of the pistol at about six o'clock on Monday morning, but there is nothing to lead to the supposition that either the man or his wife has been shot. There is reason to believe that the unfortunate man had got into difficulties, and, to some extent, this had something to do with the crime. The news spread rapidly through the town, and caused intense excitement, and during the afternoon large numbers of persons congregated in front of the house where the crime was committed.

There was to be no trial, however, and a full explanation as to why the argument turned to murder and what the argument was about would never be known, although it probably related to financial problems. This was because Hickling's body was found near to his wife's. Rather than hang himself, however, Hicking had cut his own throat. He was still alive when the police and doctor were present, and he was taken to the infirmary but from the outset it was recognized that there was only a remote chance he would live. He died the following day, without providing any further information.

The inquests recorded the only verdicts that could be given on the basis of the indisputable evidence: wilful murder against Samuel Hicking in the case of Jane Hicking and a verdict that the killer took his own life.

CHAPTER 35

An Act of Uncharacteristic Cruelty: The Murder by Patrick Kennedy 1878

A husband's frustration at his wife's drunken habits led to a bloody murder in Derby in November 1878.

At about 7pm one Saturday evening, Margaret Kennedy left her home at 9 Chapel Street to go 'marketing'. She had been confined to the house for a number of weeks due to ill health. She had not fully recovered but was no doubt in need of a break.

Margaret was accompanied by her nine-year-old daughter, Mary Jane, and was carrying her one-month-old daughter, Clara. As they left the house the mother was already very much under the influence of alcohol but she had no intention of sobering up. The mother and daughters called in at Thomas Cox's Vaults where Margaret was served 3d of rum. They then went to Baxter's Vaults where they were refused any alcohol, not because of her drunken state, but because the baby was crying. Margaret was too drunk to carry her youngest daughter by this time, so Clara was carried by Mary Jane. As they walked home, Margaret struggled to walk and fell over in Queen Street.

When they arrived home Margaret's husband, Patrick Kennedy, a thirty-six-year-old labourer, was furious at his wife's state. According to neighbours, there had never been any disturbances in the past and the couple had appeared to be quite happily married, although there had been concerns about Margaret's apparent alcoholism. There was certainly a major disturbance that night.

Chapel Street, Derby, showing the home of the Kennedy family where Patrick Kennedy brutally killed his wife in an episode of uncharacteristic violence in 1878. The author

Seemingly not normally a violent man, something inside Patrick's mind turned and he hit his wife on the side of her head, causing her to stumble and bang her head against a wall. He went to hit her again but she managed to move sufficiently to prevent another blow to the head. However, she was then kicked in her side, on the lower part of her back, knocking her to the ground.

Mary Jane fled the house to the back yard shouting, 'My father is beating my mother' but the assault continued un-interrupted in her absence, with no one coming to assist or showing any concern or interest.

Mary Jane then took Clara to her grandmother's house nearby on Walker Lane. At this time Margaret ran in the street and was seen to be heavily bleeding. Seeing what he had done, Patrick began to appear to be concerned and sent for some brandy. He had cried and seemed upset. However, whilst his wife lay dying he sent for two pints of beer for himself, some of which he threw on his wife's face before saying he wished she would go to hell.

Sketches from the *Derby Mercury* relating to the murder of Margaret Kennedy in 1878. Author's collection

Mary Ann Hardman was one of a number of women who eventually tried to help Margaret. After unsuccessfully trying to get medical help, having left a message for a doctor to come to Chapel Street, she found Margaret stood up, with her husband sat down nearby. She was told to lie down again at which point she exclaimed, 'I am dying.' Later, however, she felt she was improving in health and told Hardman, 'I am getting better now.' The initial shock and pain of her injuries may have subsided slightly, and her body's natural pain relief may have kicked in, but her condition was very much deteriorating.

It was shortly before 10pm that the surgeon, Mr Walter Goodall Copestake, finally arrived, having not been at home when called for at 9.10pm. It was quite apparent to him that there was no hope that his patient would survive for more than a few hours. He nonetheless tried to do all that he could for her. His efforts to take the dying woman upstairs to wash her wounds, proved to be unsuccessful, due largely to Kennedy's behaviour. Even as his wife lay completely defenceless he continued his attack. When the police arrived at the house one of the women who had tried attending to the dying woman exclaimed, 'I am pleased you've come in. We cannot prevent him from jumping on her.'

Upon their arrival police constables Brown and Crabbe arrested Patrick Kennedy on a charge of violent assault. This charge was to change as Margaret's health quickly deteriorated and she died at 11pm. Upon being arrested Kennedy had been violent towards the officers. Upon being charged with his wife's murder he appeared very upset although his wife's death itself did not particularly upset him, according to the police. He slept well that night but that was no doubt at least partly due to the amount of alcohol he had consumed.

On the way to the police station Kennedy told the officers it would be a bad night's work for him and asked what his children would do if he got punished. He had started to sober up by this time.

There was immense interest from the public, as word spread of the horrific event, with crowds gathering outside the house to see the blood. In Victorian England there was a morbid fascination with all things gruesome.

The inquest in the grand jury room at the Town Hall also saw crowds of people trying to catch a glimpse of the killer and hear of his cruel act of violence. There were so many people lined along the streets that the police had difficulty in maintaining a clear passage to and from the Town Hall. Those who managed to get close to hear proceedings heard evidence that the cause of death was the kick to Margaret's lower back. After a short period of deliberations the jury returned a verdict of wilful murder against Patrick Kennedy.

The jury at his trial in February 1879 agreed and found him guilty of murder. However, Kennedy was lucky and was given mercy, no doubt due to his previous good character, being spared the death penalty. Instead he was sentenced to fifteen years of penal servitude.

CHAPTER 36

Killed in the Line of Duty: The Murder of Police Constable Moss 1879

Whenever a police officer is killed there is often a more extensive and determined approach to an investigation than in the cases of murders of any typical member of society. The process by which justice is exacted is also frequently more quickly paced and a greater punishment is served to all of those involved. Few cases demonstrate this better than that which saw Gerald Mainwaring carry out an unprovoked and unnecessary crime that cost one police officer his life and which nearly killed a second officer.

Gerald Mainwaring was twenty-three years old when his trial was held on 31 July 1879. He stood accused of murdering Police Constable James Moss of Derby police force who was fatally wounded on 12 July, just nineteen days earlier. Such was the shortness of criminal procedures in the Victorian period that, if there was the necessary will to make it happen, that a murder could take place, with the completion of an inquest within little more than two weeks and a trial a few days later, with the trial lasting less than a day. This is in stark contrast to the current lengthy magistrate, committal and pre-trial hearings that can last anywhere up to a year, or even longer. Mainwaring was also charged with shooting and wounding Police Constable Price with intent to kill.

A large crowd had assembled long before the court proceedings began at 10am with Mr Lawrence QC and Horace Smith prosecuting, Mainwaring defended by the Solicitor General, Sir Hardinge Grifard QC and Mr Harris. A man of some financial means, and from a middle-class family, Mainwaring had been able to obtain legal assistance which far exceeded that of most others who had found themselves in the dock charged with murder. The judge was Mr Justice Lindley. In fact such was the level of interest that people were turned away unless they had a ticket to view the trial. Wooden barriers were also erected in the courtyard to prevent large crowds transgressing the court.

Other than a slight twitching of his mouth, Mainwaring was said to be 'wonderfully calm' as he pleaded 'not guilty'. The facts of the case were then delivered to the twelve-man jury and the very many more curious spectators.

Euphemine Dobson was a witness who told the court that Mainwaring had visited her shop on 10 July and bought a five-chambered revolver, with ivory stock and approximately 500 cartridges. He told the shop worker that he had come from America and intended to return there.

That same day Mainwaring went to The Royal Hotel and had dinner with a man. Fanny Davies told the court that she had served the men a bottle of champagne, two sherries and two whiskies. The next day Mainwaring returned with a woman called Annie Green, and they had lunch. The couple then went for a drive before returning and had dinner. They once again went out and later returned about 9pm and started to have a drinking session. They left an order for breakfast for the following day and then left for the night. On neither day had there been any trouble, even though some alcohol had been consumed. It proved to be the effects of the consumption of a greater amount of alcohol that caused Mainwaring to be transformed into a dangerous killer.

On the Saturday Fanny Davis once again served both Mainwaring and Green, shortly before noon. The couple had ordered three pints of claret, a brandy and soda, a plain soda and a quart bottle of brandy served in a decanter, which they consumed over the course of approximately four hours, leaving at about 4pm, with only approximately two teaspoons of brandy being left. Davis told the court that the 'lady seemed very drunk and the man seemed under the influence of liquor'. It was this amount of alcohol that turned Mainwaring into a murderer.

Sophie Gilbert gave evidence of the early stages of the transformation. She told the court that Mainwaring visited her home on 10 July and the following two days. On 12 July, at about 4pm, he visited with Green, after they had left The Royal Hotel. Both were noticeably different to how they had been on the previous two days, because of their drunken states. Green had fallen over and struggled to stay upright once she had got back on her feet. Mainwaring had shouted at her for being drunk, although he was seemingly no more sober than she. He asked Gilbert if he could take Green away for two or three days. Gilbert was concerned by this and refused to allow it. 'No I will not allow her to go out of the house,' she said. Unhappy by that response to his request, Mainwaring drew a revolver and began to load it, dropping some cartridges on the floor in his rush. He put his arm round Green and pointed the revolver at Gilbert who, naturally terrified, shouted, 'Take her for God's sake and go.' Henry Harrison was present during this time and he told the court that he heard the request and the refusal and had been standing near the door as Mainwaring left. The gunman had pointed the gun at Harrison and said, 'Whoever passes that door, I will shoot him.' The couple got back in the trap and Harrison was warned 'I have shot many a better than you.' Another witness also testified that he had seen Mainwaring getting on the trap with Green, with a revolver, before the trap hurriedly left.

Constable Clamp saw Mainwaring driving furiously through the streets and it was obvious to the officer that Mainwaring appeared to be under the influence of alcohol. Unaware of the exact nature of what was happening he gave chase and was joined by other officers. The chase ended at the Traveller's Rest on Ashbourne Road, where Mainwaring pulled up. He and Green were then taken into custody and put in a trap under the control of Clamp and another officer. Constable Shirley took control of the trap which Mainwaring had been driving, after refusing to accept a lift to the station from the arrested man and also having turned down Mainwaring's offer of a drink. The arrested man had tried to tell the constable that everything would be fine because his father had once been a magistrate in Stafford. He was arrested for being in control of a trap whilst under the influence of alcohol. None of the officers were aware that he was in possession of a firearm, or any of the incidents that had taken place earlier that day and no effort was made to search him. If they had known, then a life might possibly have been saved.

Clamp told the court that once she had been arrested Green became very violent. Mainwaring started using foul language and told her to be quiet. He told her that the situation would cost him £100 but the police would not know his name.

Upon arriving at the police station Green became even more abusive, violent and excited and so it was decided to deal with her first. Clamp grabbed hold of her waist and as he did so she struck him in the head. Price said, 'Come we can have no more of this.' Mainwaring meanwhile had walked behind a screen at the end of the counter, presumably to remove the gun from where he had concealed it on his person. By this point in time perhaps as little as only three or four minutes had elapsed since their arrival. With the revolver in his hand he exclaimed some obscenity and before he had finished his sentence a shot was heard, which was immediately followed by the shout of one of the officers who had been hit. 'Oh I'm shot, oh I'm shot,' Moss cried.

Price, with his arm still in a sling, told the court that after Moss had been shot, Mainwaring turned the revolver in his direction in an attempt to claim his second victim. The officer rushed towards the gunman, bobbing down his head to grab at the weapon, and was shot in the upper part of his helmet leaving two holes where the bullet had passed through. A second shot was fired, this time hitting his arm a little above his elbow as he clasped his arms around Mainwaring. 'Oh I'm shot in the arm,' he shouted. Clamp and the other officers grabbed Mainwaring before he could shoot anyone else and a fourth bullet was fired accidentally during the struggle, but it hit no one.

Following the shootings, and Mainwaring having been successfully restrained, both officers were taken to the infirmary. Inspector Spibey questioned the prisoner who was unrepentant, probably more due to the effects of the alcohol which he was very much under the influence of rather than any deep-rooted malice. He told the inspector that he was 'Jeremiah Smith, Jerusalem.' When he was told he would be charged with shooting, he said he would 'Shoot the devil.'

Colonel Delacombe, the Chief Constable, took to the witness stand and told the court that he had charged Mainwaring on the Saturday evening with shooting Moss and Price with intent to cause grievous bodily harm.

'They are not killed are they?' the prisoner asked, for the first time seemingly understanding what he had done and expressing concern about the consequences of his drunken actions. Upon being told they were still alive, Mainwaring replied, 'I can't help it. I don't know what I did. Is it serious?' He was told that it was very serious indeed for one of the officers, much to Mainwaring's distress.

The court heard that Moss died at 12.50pm the day after he was shot, at the infirmary. Delacombe had been present at the time of death, which was caused by the bullet which had entered the right side of the officer's chest before becoming lodged near his spine. Following the death he returned to the lock-up to try and charge Mainwaring with murder. He went three times before he had success. On the first attempt, at quarter past five, he was found to be drunk on his cell floor. On the second occasion he was found to be rambling incoherently. When he spoke to him on the third occasion Mainwaring 'seemed completely crushed' when told that he was going to be charged with murder. He was told, in response to a question, that Moss was unmarried, which came as some light relief for the killer. 'Thank God for that, at all events. Let me go back [to his cell].'

The Solicitor General, on behalf of the defendant, argued that the charge ought to be manslaughter not murder. He accepted that drunkenness was no excuse for killing and he could not claim that alcohol did not make him responsible and he could not argue that Mainwaring was insane, because he was not. Instead he argued that Mainwaring shot Moss and Price but that there was an absence of malice and therefore he could not be convicted of murder. 'This miserable story,' he claimed, was one which had been caused by his client becoming so drunk that he could not realize what he had done. He was leaving for America, the jury were informed, and in a folly he decided to go on a drinking spree of such a scale that he had not been sober from Thursday onwards. At the end of this spree he was 'wretchedly and hopelessly drunk'. And because Moss had not said or done anything to Mainwaring it followed that he could have no malice towards him. Therefore he had no motive or malice and so could not be found guilty of murder because a conviction for murder required proof of malicious intent.

The jury were asked, by the defence, to consider that had it not been for the excessive alcohol he had consumed, Mainwaring would not have become violent at all, let alone commit murder, and a number of those who knew him testified to his non-violent nature. The Reverend Vernon Young, rector of Whitmore, for instance, said Mainwaring was amiable and generous. Other witnesses made similar character references.

Summing up, the judge said there was no doubt Mainwaring fired the shot. There was, he suggested, a *prima facie* case of wilful murder, but the question was could it be reduced to manslaughter? He believed that a man could go and kill a total stranger and there could be malice. He expressed regret that the word 'malice' had ever been introduced into the legal world because it was ambiguous and caused embarrassment. He said the jury could not draw a distinction between murder and manslaughter in this case, and drunkenness could not be used to reduce a murder charge to manslaughter. In firing the shot, he told the jury, Mainwaring had intended to endanger the lives of others and was aware of his actions, especially taking into consideration the very fact that he was in possession of a dangerous weapon, which he had loaded and threatened the lives of a number of people with, thus proving that he was aware of what he was doing.

The jury retired to consider their verdict and after three hours and eighteen minutes of deliberations, an uncommonly long period of time during Victorian trials, they returned to find Gerald Mainwaring guilty of murder and attempted murder. They did, however, give a strong recommendation for mercy. When asked if he had anything to say, a solemn Mainwaring simply replied, 'Nothing at all.'

The judge donned the black cap and recommended that Mainwaring should make the most of his remaining time on earth, before sentencing him to death. As he did so those present noticed that the convicted killer appeared to be unmoved.

The justice system had moved at a furious pace thus far. Yet this case was far from over, with plenty more drama to follow. Following the conviction and sentencing, a sensational claim was made that rather than determine a verdict based upon the principle of twelve good men and true all agreeing on a verdict after thrashing out the evidence adhering to legal instructions, it was said that the jury at Mainwaring's trial had actually drawn lots to decide whether or not Mainwaring should be convicted of murder or manslaughter. Six of the jury members had wanted to return a verdict of wilful murder whilst the other six had thought a verdict of manslaughter was justified. This being in the days before hung juries led to retrials, and before majority verdicts were permissible, the members decided to draw lots with a man's fate resting on nothing more than the laws of chance. Cards were picked and the person who picked the blank card was the one who was allowed to decide upon which verdict should be returned. It is said, and was widely accepted to have been the case, that this method was used and the verdict reached through this method was one of manslaughter. However, a number of the members of the jury decided this was unfair and so it was decided to apply the equally unfair system of tossing a coin.

It sounds remarkable that a matter of life and death can be decided in such a way and inevitably great outrage was caused when this fact was discovered. Questions were asked in the House of Commons and a petition was drawn up calling for the death sentence to be commuted to one of life imprisonment, the majority of the signatories residing in Sheffield, with a number of the members of the jury also applying their signature to the petition.

The Home Secretary denied that the verdict could have been decided in such a way, notwithstanding the fact that the petition had been signed by some of those who had formed the jury and were therefore witnesses and participants in the alleged incident. In the Commons the Home Secretary said, 'All I can say at present is that I cannot imagine how any jury could possibly be guilty of such a diabolical act, for I cannot conceive anything more wrong, more wicked, or more absolutely calculated to supersede the code of justice.' According to the Home Secretary the claim was contradicted in a newspaper by a member of the jury and he felt confident that there was no truth in the allegation.

Irrespective of the manner in which the verdict was reached, and it seems reasonable to conclude that a game of chance did take place, and with the controversy that followed, the campaign to commute the sentence gained such popularity that immense political pressure was placed on the Home Secretary.

And so it was that the Home Secretary was forced to bow down to the pressure. His decision was received in the form of a letter dated 12 August 1879:

Sir – The Secretary of State for the Home Department having considered your application on behalf of Gerald Mainwaring, I have the satisfaction to acquaint you that he has felt warranted, under all the circumstances, in advising Her Majesty to commute the capital sentence in his case to one of penal servitude for life.

I am, Sir, your obedient servant,

A. F. Liddell.

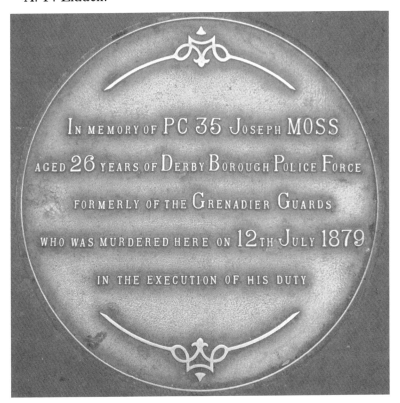

In 2002, to commemorate the death of PC Moss, a plaque was placed on the spot where he was fatally shot, in Lock Up Yard. The author

Mainwaring's life was spared, although his murder conviction still stood, but he was not the only individual involved who was prosecuted. A week after his conviction Annie Green was brought before the mayor and magistrates and fined 10s and costs for being drunk in John Taylor's premises. She pleaded guilty, claiming she recalled nothing of what happened that night. Taylor, of The Royal Hotel, was charged with a breach of the terms of his licence by having allowed Green and Mainwaring to become excessively drunk. He was fined 40s and costs or fourteen days' imprisonment with hard labour. One has to wonder how many cases of murder have taken place due to extreme intoxication, and of those how many resulted in the prosecution of the supplier of the alcohol responsible for that intoxication. There must surely be very few such prosecutions. But for the fact that the victims were two police officers, Taylor would probably never have been considered a criminal at all.

CHAPTER 37

The Result of Social Stigma: The Murder of Adeline Wright 1880

The stigma surrounding unmarried, single mothers in Victorian England requires little description. Suffice to say that Mary Wright was more fortunate than many of her peers who had fallen in the family way, with her parents allowing her to continue to live in the family home and supporting her financially as best they could. Sadly, the young mother did not receive the emotional support that could have saved the life of her child and prevented her family from being torn apart.

Wright was twenty-seven years old when she heard what for many would be considered good news, but for Wright threatened to destroy her life. She had been courting a servant of her father, who owned a farm at Bonsall, and had fallen pregnant for the second time. The servant, Henry Abell, refused to look after the mother and child upon its birth, and it was widely believed that he had also been the father of Wright's first child. That child, a daughter, was three years old and named Adeline, but was known as Addie.

When she told her father that she was pregnant again he said, 'If you do these things you must leave the house.' Unable to cope and knowing not what to do she tried to kill herself and the child.

Elizabeth Spencer lived within fifty yards of the house in which Wright's father lived and had known Wright all her life. On Sunday 4 July at about midnight, Spencer was in bed when she heard a knock at her door. When she went down she discovered it was Wright, who asked to be let in. Spencer put her hand on her shoulder and discovered the visitor was soaking wet.

Spencer's first thought or, most probably, initial hope, was that it must have been raining very heavily but upon being told that this was not the case, the horrifying truth began to become apparent.

'Have you been in the water?' Spencer asked the trembling woman. The answer was 'Yes.'

Spencer saw that Wright had her jacket on her arm and also a little blue shawl usually worn by the child and her concern began to turn to panic, with hope fading fast.

'Where is Addie?' she pleaded, being told that she was on Bonsall Moor.

When asked if Addie was in the water, the child's mother and killer answered that she was. There was no evasiveness but her replies were confined, by and large, to monosyllable answers to direct questions.

Spencer went to fetch Wright's mother, and after a few minutes the mother had come to her house. Wright's mother began to cry as Elizabeth Spencer recounted the basic facts as she understood them. The daughter knew what she had done and tried to calm her distressed mother: 'Don't cry mother. There's no one to blame but myself.'

Apportioning blame was only one matter, however. It was hoped that Addie could be found alive and that she would be okay. Wright was taken home whilst Spencer's husband and Wright's father, James Wright, set out to look out for the toddler. Approaching the mere, the body was found. Addie was dead.

Spencer went to Wright's home and asked her what had happened and found that Wright was in a better position to provide more details of what she had done, and why.

She said, 'Oh Mrs Spencer I did not throw it in. I took it in my arms and meant to die with it. People said drowning was an easy death to die but I could not die. I have been in the water two hours or more.'

Dr W H Gregory confirmed what everyone already knew, that death had been caused by drowning. There were no other signs of injury. The police arrived to speak to Wright on the night of the death but decided to make their arrest the following day, allowing Wright to have some rest. Although the medical opinion was that Wright was capable of being questioned it would appear the police had some concerns about her state.

The murder came as an obvious shock but there had been some warning signs that had been given insufficient attention, although no one could have predicted the extreme action that would occur. During the earliest court appearances Spencer said in response to Mr Skidmore, defending, that the woman had been looking unwell recently and had a strange look about her and was not as cheerful as usual.

At the trial held on 28 July 1880 her defence, led by Mr Horace Smith, argued the defendant was not guilty of murder having been temporarily insane when the crime was committed. The jury heard the testimony of Dr Webb, who had known Wright for some time, and who believed she had suffered insanity at the time of the drowning. The prosecution's witness, Dr Gregory, gave his medical opinion that she had not been insane but had suffered from 'brain fever'.

The jury heard that Mary Wright had been working in the shop but had recently stayed away and sat in her bedroom on her own. Concerned, her mother sent another daughter to sleep in the room with her, so that she was not alone.

The jury was told that James Wright found out the news of his daughter's pregnancy on that tragic Sunday, during the morning. He was told that she was pregnant, supposedly by the same man, and he told her that she was disgracing him again and would have to leave. She said she would go but stayed in the house until the evening, at which time she left without saying anything to her mother or sister. She may not have spoken to her mother, but she did leave her a note:

Dear Mother – I leave this note, as you will not see me alive again or my child. I am pregnant by Henry Abell, which you know. You will think it strange about the child but I could not leave it. I have left home of my own will, which you are not responsible for. M Wright.'

She then took the child in her arms, walked to her father's fields where there was a mere for watering cattle, approximately one yard deep in the middle. She was seen at between 7 and

8pm, by her father, walking along the road to the moor with Addie. When she had reached the mire, she stood in the water and there she drowned her daughter.

There was no dispute that Wright had killed Addie. Did the defence's argument, that she had suffered insanity as a result of depression and feeling dejected, and the attempt of ending her own life and her successful attempt at ending her daughter's life, was triggered by her father forcing her to leave the house have any truth? She was faced with a difficult problem in that unable to live in the family home, and with no financial support, she would have had to live in poverty, unable to provide for herself or her children. It was accepted by both defence and prosecution counsels that she was sane at the time of the trial.

The jury did not believe that she had been insane and found her guilty of murder, but strongly recommended mercy. The judge, Baron Huddleston, passed the death sentence but did not don the black cap. A panel of twelve married matrons determined she was indeed pregnant and that she would give birth before long. Sentence was delayed until she had given birth but it was never carried out. Her death sentence was commuted to one of ten years of penal servitude. After serving only seven years at Millbank Penitentiary and Woking women's prison, Mary Wright was released on 20 March 1887 and returned to the farm to live with the father whose earlier rejection had resulted in such devastation.

CHAPTER 38

A Young Life Cut Short: The Murder of Eliza Wilkinson 1880

A wicked and evil crime was committed in Derby in the spring of 1880, which saw a young girl brutally murdered for reasons that will never be fully understood.

Eliza Wilkinson was only nine years old when, on 26 April, she was out with an older sister, Elizabeth, who was sixteen years old, selling comb boxes made by their father at half a penny each. The sisters left their home, 67 Bridge Street, at about 9am and went from door to door in order to try and sell their fourteen boxes of combs. At about 11am the girls went into Green Street and Eliza was given a comb box to try selling on her own. It will never be known if, had she been accompanied by Elizabeth, her life would not have then ended or if there would have been two victims.

Eliza went to Tan Yard, off Green Street, taking no money with her, carrying just the box. Eliza spoke to a number of people as she tried, unsuccessfully, to sell her box. Elizabeth wondered what had happened to her when she had not returned a short while later.

At 11am Elizabeth went home alone and asked her father, James, if Eliza had returned. 'We had but two boxes left and I was trying to sell one on one side of the street and Eliza on the other side,' Elizabeth explained to her father. He told Elizabeth and her younger brother, who shared his father's name, to go and find her, which they did. A resident informed the two children that Eliza had tried selling her a comb and had then gone into the inner court. They asked other residents and a woman told the youngsters six words, which must have left them shocked and distraught: 'A man has killed your sister.'

By this point in time the police had arrived at the home of John Wakefield, a twenty-eight-year-old labourer who lived with his mother and brother, and the two children made their way to the Tan Yard to see what was happening. A short while later James returned home and told his father 'A man has got Eliza in a house.' No doubt he did not believe that his sister had been killed.

The father and son hurriedly made their way to Tan Yard and the awful truth was discovered when they saw Eliza lying on the floor of Wakefield's house, in a pool of blood. Her throat had been cut and she was dead.

The killer had given himself up at about 11.30am according to Inspector George Barnes or prior to 11.15am according to Delacombe. After slitting the girl's throat, Wakefield went to the police station asking for the superintendent and upon being asked why he wished to see him he responded, 'I have committed a murder,' but he was not believed at first.

'Surely you are not one of those kind of men who are fond of fallacies to give yourself up for murder,' he had been asked, by a sceptical officer. 'It is not a fallacy. It is true,' the killer had replied. The reason for the scepticism was that the manner in which Wakefield spoke was so cool and calm that it did not appear that he was making a genuine confession.

Lieutenant Colonel Delacombe was sent for and the killer advised that they should go and see for themselves that a murder had been committed. Delacombe and two officers (Detective Inspector Spibey and Assistant Inspector Jackson) went to the house and found the body. The door was locked but the key was on the window ledge and they let themselves in. Eliza was found in a pool of blood lying on her back in the left hand corner of a room at the foot of a flight of stairs to the bedroom. Her hat was on her head, fastened beneath her chin with a piece of plastic. She was still warm but very clearly dead. A worn table knife lay beside her and a half penny was in her hand. A comb box was on the table. A bowl containing bloody water suggested that Wakefield had tried to clean up before giving up and giving himself up. His shirt sleeves were found to be stained with blood.

Eliza's throat had been cut in four places. Two of the wounds were major and two were relatively minor. A further cut was located on the shoulder blade. Her knees were also bruised. There was no evidence of sexual assault.

When taken to the lock-up and later charged with murder Wakefield said he had nothing to say and refused to comment on his crime to Delacombe other than that which he had earlier said that he had committed a murder.

There was no evidence to suggest Wakefield knew the deceased. She had no money or worthy goods on her. Her only possessions on her person, when she entered the house, were a pill box containing some oats and the box of combs, which seemingly Wakefield had paid for. There appeared to be no motive, unless Wakefield had intended to rape or sexually assault the nine-year-old, but panicked and killed her, or killed her when she struggled.

At Wakefield's trial at the Summer Assizes, the defendant pleaded 'not guilty' to the murder. Mr Stanger, for the defence, claimed his client had killed whilst suffering from insanity. Under cross-examination the gaol surgeon, Dr Wright Baker, said that it was true that a degree of mania could manifest itself in Wakefield without warning. He added that if no motive could be found he would believe it was possible that Wakefield killed as a result of homicidal mania and therefore he was not responsible for his actions and would be guilty of manslaughter on the grounds of insanity rather than murder. In response to a question from the judge he said that the form of mania he was referring to was that known as kleptomania, an incontrollable impulse but that the person would be aware of what they were doing but powerless to stop themselves.

Summing up, the judge, Mr Baron Huddleston, told the jury that everyone was sane until proven otherwise and that they had to be sure whether the prisoner was aware of what he was doing and whether he knew it was wrong. He explained to the jury the difference between murder and manslaughter. The judge said there was no evidence of 'hereditary taint' and no evidence of insanity in the defendant's medical history. The jury agreed and did not even have to leave their box to properly discuss the evidence. They were no doubt horrified and appalled by such a heinous crime against someone so young who should have had a lifetime ahead of her. Wakefield was found guilty of murder and duly sentenced to death, a sentence which was carried out on 16 August 1880 while a large crowd waited outside the prison for the black flag to be raised, marking the fact the execution had taken place. By this time executions were not allowed to be witnessed by the public (the last public hanging had taken place twelve years earlier) but this did not deter large numbers of people gathering at the places of lawful execution to be near to the hangings whilst they were being carried out, even if they could not actually see them. Each execution would, however, be witnessed by representatives of the media who were allowed to report on them.

It is often the case that killers who have committed such grave acts of violence have committed previous, relatively minor offences, which have escalated to murder. Although the precise details could not be found during the writing of this book, this is certainly the case for John Wakefield who was convicted in 1871, nine years before he killed Eliza Wilkinson, of assaulting a young child. One has to wonder whether, if he had been given greater punishment for the earlier attack and if rehabilitation had been attempted during the Victorian period, the murder of Eliza Wilkinson would have been prevented.

CHAPTER 39

Nursing to Death: The Crimes of Elizabeth Berry 1886

When Mary Ann Finley died in February 1886 it was thought that death was natural, that she had had a stroke, but a year later doubts caused an investigation which led to an entirely different conclusion.

Following revelations about the death of Mrs Finley's granddaughter, the Home Secretary ordered that Mary Finley's body should be exhumed. In February 1887, Elizabeth Berry was convicted of killing her eleven-year-old daughter Edith, who died of poisoning on 4 January that year, in order to cash in a life insurance policy. She had denied the murder, which took place in Oldham, but the evidence was overwhelming that the thirty-one-year-old had given her daughter a milky fluid containing a corrosive poison, which had caused an agonising death.

As a consequence of Edith's death, and her mother's conviction for it, there were suspicions that Berry had committed further murders, including that of her mother, Mary Ann Finley, who similarly had life insurance taken out for her and who suddenly died. Berry's date of execution was postponed until the further deaths could be investigated. There were suspicions Berry had murdered her second husband and son, who died suspiciously within fourteen months of each other, between 1882 and 1884, but those deaths were never officially attributed to her and she never stood trial for them.

At the time of her mother's death, Elizabeth Berry had been staying at Finley's home, 4 Back Albion Street, Castleton.

The post-mortem examination following exhumation revealed no traces of poison in Finley's body, although examination of the stomach and intestines did reveal traces of a substance extracted from deadly nightshade. The examiner, Mr Paul of Liverpool, could not determine how much of the substance had been administered and thought that much of the administered dose may have disappeared in the year that had elapsed between death and burial, and the exhumation and post mortem. 'The amount extracted was very small, but a small quantity is a fatal dose,' he told the inquest, which was held in March 1887 at the Blue Pits Inn, Castleton. Death, he said, would have followed great heat and dryness of the throat, convulsions and insensibility. Unlike mineral poisons there would have been no effects to be seen following death, or at least none that could be detected in late Victorian times.

Evidence was also provided relating to the deceased's medical history in the weeks prior to her death. On 27 January, a surgeon had visited the dying woman and had noted she had a severe attack of nosebleeds. Three days later he visited again and did so a further time, on 6 February, when Finley was suffering from palpitations and sleeplessness. He continued to visit until her death. During one of his visits he saw his patient have a fit and on 9 February or 10 February he noted that she was suffering from convulsions. She had been hysterical early on and had been prescribed morphine but it had become clear her condition was quickly deteriorating. The surgeon had originally attributed the hysteria to her having taken too much spirit which he had prescribed when in reality it was probably one of the symptoms of atropia, a toxic alkaloid extracted from members of the nightshade family of plants which can cause delirium, a dry mouth, urinary retention and flushed and hot skin. He was of the opinion, having assisted with the post mortem, that the deceased had not died of natural causes as he had originally believed, having certified that death was the consequence of 'cerebral haemorrhage and coma'. However, he claimed at the inquest that at no time had he seen her eyes dilated which one would expect had she been administered the poison from which she was alleged to have died.

Dr Thomas Harris, a pathologist who exhumed the corpse and assisted with the post mortem, claimed the body, which had been buried with a Rochdale newspaper wrapped around it, was very badly decomposed. He could not conclusively determine the cause of death. There were no visible indications of disease that could have caused death, although he acknowledged some traces of disease can disappear after a year and also the state of the body made the post mortem difficult. Upon being asked whether he thought the symptoms as described by the doctor who visited the deceased before death were consistent with poisoning he said, 'Quite so. Not only consistent, but very suspicious of atropia poisoning,' despite the eyes having not been dilated.

Elizabeth Berry had, at the time she began staying with her mother, recently gained a position as a nurse working at the Chesterfield workhouse. She obtained the position on 23 January 1886 and commenced her employment on 1 February. The following day, however, she ceased to work there, claiming that she needed to look after her mother. On 5 February, the Clerk to the Guardians of the Chesterfield Union received a letter stating, 'Sir – My mother is sinking very fast, so that it will be impossible for me to leave her. Will you please present the enclosed to your Board at the next meeting?' The enclosed document was a formal letter of resignation on the grounds that her mother was 'dangerously ill'.

Sarah Pombert was able to offer further evidence that Finley had died from atropia poisoning. Pombert was the deceased's sister, who had received a telegram on 11 February stating 'Mrs Walsh is dangerously ill. If you want to see her, come at once. B Berry.' Walsh was the name that Mary Finley was known by (perhaps it was her maiden name). This had come as a shock because there had been no previous indications that Finley had been in poor health. When Pombert arrived she found her sister appeared in better health than anticipated. That same evening Berry went out for an hour and a half, claiming she had to go to Rochdale, and during that time Pombert stayed by her sister's bedside, where she remained all night. The following night Berry refused to allow the visitor to be beside her sister. Finley asked that her niece be requested to come, so a telegram was sent to Manchester and the niece duly arrived.

Berry again went to Rochdale that evening and when she returned she brought with her a type of jelly-looking substance which she gave to Finley in a tea cup. Upon tasting it the deceased said she did not like it and pushed it away. Later that day she showed some slight signs of an improvement. She was more cheerful and promised to go and visit her sister and niece when she was feeling strong enough. She had complained about being very thirsty, however, suffering from a very dry mouth.

Sarah Pombert had understandably been concerned about her sister's health and upon asking Berry what the doctor had thought, she was told, 'Oh he thinks there is a great deal of brain mischief at work.' Upon being asked what she thought of her mother's condition, Berry answered 'I think she is sinking.'

The following morning Pombert woke up between 4 and 5 and saw Berry at her door. 'Aunt are you coming?' she was asked, before being told that there had been a change for the worse in Finley's health.

The sister ran downstairs and saw her sister on her back, twitching, with her hands trembling and she appeared to be flushed. She did not speak and it was not long before she died.

Once the cause of death had been concluded as poisoning, following the post mortem, a witness was found who was able to provide evidence that a woman, believed to be Mrs Berry, had purchased an ounce and a half of solution of atropia from a chemists at Rochdale on the two separate evenings that Berry is known to have gone to Rochdale. The customer used the false name Ellen Saunders of Castleton. She did, however, inform the chemist that she was a nurse. She had trained as a nurse at Manchester Infirmary and had worked at Oldham Infirmary at the time of Edith's death.

The motive was quite clear. Berry had insured her mother's life for £100 in 1882 with the Wesleyan and General Insurance Society, with her being the beneficiary in the event of death. She applied for the money before it was due, claiming she had to go to Australia as a nurse or companion of an invalid. The sum of £100 minus 16s 8d (interest due to being paid in advance) was given to her. Berry had also insured her mother for more than £13 with the Rational Sick and Burial Society.

It took only a few minutes for the inquest jury to return a verdict of wilful murder against Elizabeth Berry, who had been described in the press as being a 'very clever, accomplished, fascinating woman who can play and sing'. Having already been convicted of murdering Edith Berry, any trial for the murder of Mary Finley was merely academic and to satisfy procedures but a conviction for Finley's murder did follow. Berry was hanged at Walton Prison in Liverpool, the first person to have had her life ended at that place of lawful execution, on 14 March 1887.

CHAPTER 40

A Perfect Murder or Senseless Suicide? The Death of James Jacques 1889

ames Jacques was a sixty-nine-year-old framework knitter and was known to have had some savings and property. He had lived alone in one of his cottages at Horsley Woodhouse for four years, with his two sons William and Joseph living together in Clay Cross along with William's wife, their children and the mother-in-law. There had been no signs of any great problems in Jacques' life but on the morning of 29 September he was found lying dead on the floor of his home, with his throat cut. A small sharp knife covered in blood was found in his hand.

It may have appeared, at first, to be a case of suicide and it was no doubt the intention of the killer to give the false impression that suicide had taken place, but such a theory was dismissed reasonably quickly, partly because of the angle at which the wound was inflicted but also largely because of the identification of someone who had motive to kill the elderly man.

William Jacques told the police of suspicions he had against his brother. Joseph, who was aged about twenty-five years, had allegedly, in the past, once asked William if he would help murder their father to inherit his money. He had supposedly said that they should visit their father's house one Saturday night when he was in bed and they would surprise him, cut his throat and steal his money. William had rebuked his brother for such an idea and it was not talked about again and was probably not taken as a serious comment. William did not believe his father was in any danger because Joseph would require another individual in order to enact his murderous plot and he did not think his brother would be able to find someone willing to commit such a crime. It appears that William never informed his father of this alleged conversation.

Joseph's movements on the night of the murder were scrutinised. Joseph claimed he had last seen his father on Wednesday 25 September and had not been anywhere near James' home on the Saturday night or early hours of Sunday morning. That night Joseph had been out of the house, having left at 2pm in the afternoon, and did not return until about 3.30am. William had waited up for him, unaware at that time that their father had been killed, and when Joseph returned he was seen to appear pale, agitated and 'peculiar'. He was drunk and said he had been drinking in Chesterfield at Fox's Vaults where he arrived before 8pm, having caught the 6.48pm train from Clay Cross to Chesterfield. According to his account he had several drinks and left Chesterfield at about 3am.

Subsequent investigations failed to identify anyone who could corroborate Joseph's story. The only witnesses who had encountered him were only able to say that Joseph had spoken of going to Chesterfield but there was no proof he had actually made that journey. However, equally there were no witnesses to place him in the Horsley Woodhouse area.

One of James' neighbours, Joseph Lovatt, a fellow frame-work knitter, saw the deceased at 8.45pm on the Saturday night. Although James was busy at work, the neighbour stayed with him for approximately an hour and had no reason for any concern when he left.

Another neighbour, Mary Radcliffe, had seen James' home illuminated at 11.30pm, with the sound of his machinery clearly audible. She retired to bed at midnight and the only sound she heard emanating from James's home was what sounded like a plank falling over. The time was sadly never stated, if Radcliffe was ever aware of it. Was this singular sound associated with James Jacques' death, which would suggest a lack of any argument or struggle, or did he die later, whilst Radcliffe was asleep? It would appear that the murder was committed in the early hours of the Sunday morning.

The body was found by Hannah Woolin at about 8am. She went each morning to take James his milk. She had seen the stairfoot door was partly open, which was unusual, and upon pushing it further open she saw James on the floor in a pool of blood.

In his defence it was argued that Joseph had not committed murder and indeed no one had. The first doctor to examine the body, Dr Garnham, believed it to be a case of probable suicide, which is why no one heard any struggle, screaming or raised voices, and it was this finding that was relied upon by Joseph. It was his opinion that the wound must have been inflicted by James' own hand or by someone from behind acting very carefully to produce a clean, neat cut. Dr Woolley, of Heanor, however, had made a careful examination and found it would be impossible for him to have slit his own throat given that the knife was turned away from his neck and so the killer must have placed the knife in his hand following the murder to give the false impression of suicide.

William Jacques had informed the authorities and the inquest jury that his father had no reason to commit suicide. He had been of usual health and quite lively, William recalled, although he had not seen his father since 14 August. He accepted that his father had felt lonely on occasions.

There was very little evident disturbance when Police Constable George Murray inspected the scene. There were some copper coins scattered across the floor in the room in which James' body was found and there were bloodstains of finger marks on the dresser. There were some tools and objects in a drawer covered in blood which was interpreted as suggesting the victim had been leaning over the drawer when his throat was cut. Elsewhere in the building, however, there was no disturbance and no evidence for anything having been stolen.

The jury rejected the suicide theory and returned a verdict of wilful murder by person or persons unknown but that there was strong suspicion against Joseph Jacques. The coroner, however, refused to add the latter part to the verdict because there had been insufficient evidence against him to allow it to be recorded by law and because suspicions were not enough to formally accuse an individual.

The police had, however, formally accused Joseph Jacques of patricide. On the basis of his brother's information he had been charged with wilful murder and had been remanded into custody. Indeed, during the inquest he was present during proceedings as a prisoner. Although the magistrates accepted there was a lack of material evidence against him, they believed that there was sufficient reason for Joseph to stand trial for murder even though by that time William Jacques had withdrawn his claim that his brother had plotted to kill their father. Had William fabricated the claim against his brother or did he feel guilty about condemning a man for murder based on a story that may have been little more than a foolish bravado and one which he had no intention of committing? The truth is probably that he did indeed doubt that his brother was guilty after having been subjected to cross examination at the inquest and magistrates' hearing.

When questioned about the night of 28/29 September, William accepted that he did not see any blood on his brother's clothing or body. He had a light in his room and he had shared a bed with his brother that night. He had seen his brother undressed and noticed no marks on his body.

There were sufficient doubts to prevent the case from being fully explored at trial. On 14 October 1889, the Public Prosecutor ruled at the Ripley Petty Sessions that there was no evidence connecting Joseph Jacques to the murder of his father. He was immediately discharged and walked free to continue his life.

Who killed James Jacques and why? Were the suspicions against Joseph justified? If they were, if William had informed his father of his sibling's murderous idea, would the crime have been prevented? Or could some other unknown individual have been responsible for this grisly deed? All that is known is that Jacques did not commit suicide and no one was ever held to account for his death.

CHAPTER 41

Murder on the Barge: The Beastly Murder by John Cotton 1898

ohn Cotton was a brute of a man by anyone's standards while influenced by alcohol. He had boasted to some that he had killed his first two wives, who had both died years earlier, through sustained cruelty rather than any individual act of violence, which cut their lives short. He once threw one of his previous wives out and set fire to all the furniture. He repeatedly assaulted his wives, often in a drunken rage. He was occasionally put before magistrates charged with drunken behaviour and other minor offences and by all accounts he was a thoroughly bad man. Hannah Cotton's suffering was more swift, although torturous nonetheless. The marriage was certainly not a case of third time lucky for the elderly chap who, despite his age, was considered to be a dangerous savage of a man. His last wife was to become one of the last women to be murdered in Victorian Derbyshire in such horrific conditions.

A native of Penkridge, near Stafford, Cotton was thought by many to be sixty-four years old. Illiterate, he had worked on the canal from an early age and it was on the canal that he lived with Hannah, on a narrow boat at the Bugsworth Basin at the terminus of the Peak Forest Canal in the Derbyshire village of Buxworth. Hannah Cotton was said to be thirty years his junior. Due largely to the age difference, Cotton had many insecurities about his marriage and he would often become jealous when his wife was in the company of other men. However, Hannah appears to have been entirely loyal to the man who became a beast whilst under the influence of drink, with whom she had become tied. The landlord of the Rose and Crown, Thomas

Hayes, and his wife said that if Hannah ever so much as spoke to a man Cotton would make his displeasure known and a quarrel would follow.

On Wednesday 26 October 1898, one of their quarrels took place. That day the couple had been drinking in the Rose and Crown Inn but neither appeared to be particularly drunk when they left, although they were accompanied to their boat by the landlord. Hayes claimed this was not because they were drunk but because they had been quarrelling in the pub and he was concerned that there could be some violence. He left when he believed they were on better terms and returned to the inn. Apparently a threat had been made by Cotton to his wife but upon accompanying them to their home, the landlord believed it was an idle threat. He was very wrong.

A group of schoolgirls were to learn that the threat was far from idle. As they stood on the opposite side of the canal they witnessed what was to, no doubt, traumatise them and leave lasting impressions that must surely have haunted them for their whole lives. The cabin door was open and there was a dim light to allow the girls, Elizabeth Copeland, Selina Hall and Hilda Hayes, to see what was happening.

The girls heard screams and saw Cotton striking his wife several times about the head. An iron rod used as a poker, approximately a yard in length, was the weapon of choice. The girls ran to the Rose and Crown for assistance. As he walked along the canal, a farmer and landowner by the name of James Carrington also saw Cotton attacking his wife. According to Carrington, he heard the murderer tell his wife that he had already had two wives and would want yet another because he was tired of this one. Cotton shouted at his wife and said if she did not stop moaning he would throw her in the canal. When assistance came she was unconscious and was carried away. She died a few hours later having never regained consciousness.

The boat was a gruesome sight for those who had the displeasure of having to see it; its cabin walls were covered in blood. The weapon was found at the scene coated in blood and with hair adhered to it. A post-mortem examination was carried out by Dr Allen and Dr Anderson, who confirmed death had been caused as a result of the head injuries, amongst which was a fracture to the base of the skull, resulting in concussion of the brain.

The killer was unrepentant, no doubt at least partly due to his state of intoxication, a state which he sought to develop further. He spent the next few hours, as his wife lay dying, back drinking at the Rose and Crown and allegedly other pubs. When Mrs Hayes told Cotton that he had probably killed his wife, Cotton was said to have told her 'If you don't hold your tongue I'll serve you the same as I served her.'

That same night he was arrested by Police Constable Whitley for attempted murder. The following morning, by which time the unfortunate woman had died, the charge was upgraded to one of murder. As he sobered up Cotton began to realise the position he was now in.

At trial before Sir J C Mathew, he was defended by the son of a leading judge, Mr Justice Lawrence, but the barrister's reputation and associations were insufficient to prevent what was seen to be inevitable and true justice for the wicked crime perpetrated. Mr Lawrence's argument to reduce the charge to manslaughter failed on the basis that Cotton's violence could not be blamed on alcohol and it was accepted that he had acted with intentional malice to end his wife's life.

The jury took just quarter of an hour to return a guilty verdict for murder and they gave no recommendation of mercy. Donning the black cap, the judge told Cotton to spend his remaining time on earth preparing for judgment day and ordered that he be executed. It was reported that Cotton barely reacted to these words, having leaned on the railings of the dock and exhibited little emotion upon being told he would be hanged by the neck until he was dead. He left the dock in a cool manner.

CANAL BOAT TRAGEDY IN DERBYSHIRE.
VERDICT OF WILFUL MURDER.

Mr. Charles Davis, Coroner for the High Peak Division, held an inquest in the Church School, Bugsworth, Derbyshire, on Saturday afternoon, touching the death of Hannah Cotton, aged 36 years, wife of John Cotton, boatman, which took place as the result of injuries received during a quarrel on the previous Wednesday, on a canal boat, at Bugsworth, near Chapel-en-le-Frith. Both were in charge of the canal boat Annie, belonging to the Boulton Limekilns, Kidsgrove, Staffordshire, which had come to Bugsworth for a load of limestone. The boat was laden with limestone the same day, and was got ready for returning. Both had been drinking together. During the evening an alarm was raised that a quarrel had ensued on the canal boat.

How a local newspaper reported the 'willful murder' verdict on the death of Hannah Cotton. Author's collection

The Home Secretary looked at the case, as was the usual practice, and found no reason why the man should not be hanged despite some believing his age should warrant clemency. In this case not only was there debate over whether the crime was one of murder of manslaughter, but also the killer's age was disputed. It was, as has been said, commonly believed that Cotton was sixty-four years old. However, at his inquest at Derby Gaol held two hours after execution (inquests were held for those who were executed because their deaths were not natural and it was a legal requirement to ensure that execution had been in line with regulations), it was argued he was in fact seventy-four, whereas one witness informed the coroner, Mr W Harvey Whiston, he was seventy-one. At trial it had been said he was sixty-four and the police investigated and concluded he was sixty-five which is the age the Home Secretary was given. The inquest however ruled that for the sake of argument and in the absence of definite proof, he was seventy. Indeed it appears, from studies of the census, that he was indeed seventy-one years old. One has to wonder whether, had his true age of seventy-one been given to the Home Secretary (rather than sixty-four), greater consideration may have been paid to the application for clemency, although older killers were hanged without so much as a second thought.

For all his cold brutality during his life, and his alleged nonchalance following his crime and during his trial and sentencing, Cotton did show some remorse in the lead up to the fateful day in which he was executed. He spent some time with the prison chaplain, the Reverend J Hart Johnson, and was given the sacrament on the day before he was hanged. That same day, in the afternoon, he was visited by his two sons and a daughter and showed an element of sorrow. He informed them he had made his peace with God.

On the eve of his execution he slept badly. He rose at 5.30am on Wednesday 21 December to begin his last day on earth and had his final breakfast of tea with bread and butter. At 7am he was visited by the chaplain to prepare to be plunged into eternity.

At 7.57am representatives of the Sheriff came to the cell and told him the sentence of death was to be carried out. The chief warder led, carrying a black wand, with Cotton following, supported by two warders, and two further warders followed. The Governor, Acting Under Sheriff, the Sheriff's Officer and prison surgeon then followed. They were met halfway along the fifty-yard walk to the gallows by the chaplain reciting the burial service. Cotton walked with some difficulty. The executioner, Billington of Bolton, who was assisted by his son, stopped them before the scaffold to begin the pinioning process, fastening Cotton's hands behind his back with the son loosening the condemned man's shirt collar. Cotton appeared pale and haggard, according to the five reporters from the press who were present for the execution. They then entered the shed in which the scaffold was located. His ankles were bound together and the noose placed over his neck, with a white cap pulled over his head. The lever was then pulled with a 6ft drop at the same moment as the Chaplain said, 'Oh Lord, remember not the offences of Thy servant.' Death was, in the opinion of Dr Greaves, instantaneous.

A large crowd, a big proportion of which were women, had assembled outside the prison on that December morning to be part of the spectacle of justice that was being carried out. Unlike most other executions where at least some of those within the crowd called for a prisoner to be spared from execution, or gave pity or prayer for the convict's soul, it appears that no such calls were made for Cotton, such was the public's anger and contempt for this particular wife killer. Two policemen were present to control the crowd but there was no disorder. At 8am the black flag rose to show the execution was over and that the murderer had shared the fate of his wife. He was the last man to be hanged at Derby Gaol and the first execution since August 1895. Following death he was buried at the front wall of the prison, his body covered with quick lime as was the custom for those who met with the hangman in Derbyshire during the eighteenth and nineteenth centuries.

Sources

Local newspapers, including the *Derby and Chesterfield Reporter*, the *Derby Mercury*, the *Sheffield and Rotherham Independent* and the *Manchester Guardian*.

Lane, Brian (Ed), *Murder Club Guide to the Midlands: True Tales of Dark Deeds and Arch Fiends*, 1980

Merrill, John N, *Punishment in Derbyshire*, 1987

Index